UNIVERSAL ORLANDO

TRAVEL GUIDE

2025

Ultimate Adventure to a Seamless and Memorable Traveling with Top Attraction, Hotels, and Beaches

BY

NEWMAN S. JACKSON

Gratitude

Thank you for choosing this travel guide for your journey to Universal Orlando Resort. Your support means the world, and I am truly grateful to have been a part of your adventure planning. I hope this guide helps you create unforgettable memories and discover all the magic this incredible destination has to offer. Wishing you a fantastic and seamless trip filled with fun, excitement, and joy!

Disclaimer

The information in this guide is for general purposes only. While efforts have been made to ensure accuracy, the publisher and author are not responsible for any changes to prices, services, or policies after publication. Always verify details with Universal Orlando Resort or relevant vendors before making travel plans.

A Little Travel Humor

Why did the traveler bring a ladder to Universal Orlando Resort?

Because they heard the rides were "out of this world!"

But don't worry, no ladders needed—just this guide for an unforgettable adventure!

TABLE OF CONTENTS

Introduction..5

    Welcome to Universal Orlando Resort...5

    Why People Travel to Universal Orlando Resort..5

    History and Cultural Background of Universal Orlando Resort....................6

    Geographic and Regional Overview of Universal Orlando Resort...............6

    What's New at Universal Orlando Resort.. 7

Chapter 1: Planning and Preparation.. **8**

    Best Times to Visit Universal Orlando Resort...8

    Visa, Entry Requirements, and Procedures for Universal Orlando Resort....... 9

    Budgeting and Packing Essentials for Universal Orlando Resort............... 10

    Safety, Security, and Health Tips for Universal Orlando Resort................. 11

    Language and Communication at Universal Orlando Resort.......................13

Chapter 2: Sustainable and Responsible Travel.....................................**14**

    Environmental Preservation and Local Etiquette at Universal Orlando Resort...............14

    Travel Dos and Don'ts at Universal Orlando Resort................................. 15

    Minimizing Your Carbon Footprint at Universal Orlando Resort................ 17

    Avoiding Scams and Tourist Traps at Universal Orlando Resort............... 18

    Insider Tips for Budgeting and Money Saving at Universal Orlando Resort...................20

Chapter 3: Getting Around and Navigating Universal Orlando Resort...........................**22**

    Arriving and Departing Universal Orlando Resort.....................................22

    Local Transportation Options for Universal Orlando Resort...................... 24

    Transportation Tips for Universal Orlando Resort......................................27

    Maps and Navigation Tools for Universal Orlando Resort.........................30

Chapter 4: Where to Stay..**34**

    Accommodation Options by Budget for Universal Orlando Resort..............34

    Neighborhood Guides for Universal Orlando Resort................................. 37

    Family-Friendly Accommodations Near Universal Orlando Resort.............42

    Inclusive and LGBTQ+ Friendly Stays Near Universal Orlando Resort.........46

    Unique Stays and Experiences Near Universal Orlando Resort................50

Chapter 5: Experiencing Universal Orlando Resort................................**55**

    Must-See Attractions and Landmarks Near Universal Orlando Resort...........55

    Activities and Experiences Near Universal Orlando Resort.......................59

    Festivals and Events in Orlando.. 64

    Nightlife and Entertainment in Orlando...68

    Shopping and Souvenirs in Orlando.. 71

Chapter 6: Practical Information for Travelers..**75**

Currency, Money Matters, and Travel Insurance in Orlando.............................75

Dining and Cuisine in Orlando...78

safety tips for Solo, Group, and LGBTQ+ Travelers in Orlando, with advice tailored to each group...81

Wellness and Relaxation Options..84

Useful Contacts and Emergency Information... 87

Money matters: currency exchange and budgeting tips.................................. 90

Final tips for a successful trip...93

Themed itineraries (family, adventure, solo). Give equally the Locations, costs, contacts, etiquettes... 95

Checklist for travelers (packing, documents, etc.).. 98

Basic Questions for Every Traveler.. **102**

Universal Orlando Resort Travel Guide... 107

Introduction

Welcome to Universal Orlando Resort

Discover the ultimate vacation destination where imagination meets adventure. Universal Orlando Resort offers thrilling theme parks, world-class entertainment, and unique experiences that cater to visitors of all ages. Home to iconic attractions like The Wizarding World of Harry Potter, jaw-dropping roller coasters, and immersive shows, the resort guarantees unforgettable memories. Whether you're a movie buff, thrill-seeker, or family traveler, Universal Orlando is your gateway to excitement and fun.

Website: universalorlando.com
Contact: +1-407-363-8000

Why People Travel to Universal Orlando Resort

Universal Orlando Resort is a magnet for thrill-seekers, families, and entertainment enthusiasts. Visitors are drawn to its:

1. The Wizarding World of Harry Potter: Step into Hogwarts, Hogsmeade, and Diagon Alley to experience the magic of Harry Potter like never before.

2. Thrilling Theme Parks: Explore Universal Studios Florida, Islands of Adventure, and Volcano Bay for rides, shows, and attractions.

3. Blockbuster Rides: Experience adrenaline-pumping rides inspired by movies like Jurassic Park, Transformers, and Despicable Me.

4. Exceptional Entertainment: Enjoy live shows, parades, and nighttime spectaculars.

5. Dining and Shopping: Savor themed restaurants, character dining, and shop for exclusive merchandise.

Whether for the adventure, family bonding, or cinematic nostalgia, Universal Orlando Resort delivers unforgettable experiences.

Website: universalorlando.com
Contact: +1-407-363-8000

History and Cultural Background of Universal Orlando Resort

Universal Orlando Resort opened in 1990 with the debut of Universal Studios Florida, designed to immerse guests in the magic of movies and television. Over the years, it expanded to include Islands of Adventure in 1999 and Volcano Bay in 2017, transforming it into a multi-park destination.

The resort's cultural influence is rooted in Hollywood's storytelling, with attractions inspired by blockbuster franchises like Jurassic Park, Harry Potter, and Marvel Comics. Universal Orlando reflects a blend of cinematic innovation, creativity, and entertainment, making it a premier global destination.

Website: universalorlando.com
Contact: +1-407-363-8000

Geographic and Regional Overview of Universal Orlando Resort

Universal Orlando Resort spans over 541 acres in Orlando, Florida. It is divided into three main parks:

1. Universal Studios Florida: Focuses on movie-inspired rides, shows, and attractions.

2. Islands of Adventure: Offers thrill rides and themed areas like Jurassic Park, Marvel Super Hero Island, and The Wizarding World of Harry Potter – Hogsmeade.

3. Volcano Bay: A water theme park featuring slides, wave pools, and a relaxing tropical environment.

The resort also includes Universal CityWalk, a dining and entertainment hub, and on-site hotels catering to diverse budgets and preferences.

Orlando's warm climate and welcoming atmosphere make it a year-round destination. Visitors are encouraged to respect the family-friendly environment and adhere to safety regulations.

Website: universalorlando.com
Contact: +1-407-363-8000

What's New at Universal Orlando Resort

1. Villain-Con Minion Blast (2023): An interactive gaming experience in Universal Studios Florida, inviting guests to join the Minions on a mischievous adventure.

2. Epic Universe (Opening in 2025): A highly anticipated fourth theme park under construction, promising brand-new worlds and immersive experiences.

3. Seasonal Events: New offerings for Halloween Horror Nights, Mardi Gras celebrations, and holiday festivities.

4. Updated Dining Options: Fresh culinary experiences, including themed restaurants at CityWalk and inside the parks.
5. Park Technology Enhancements: Upgraded Virtual Line systems and mobile app features to improve convenience and wait times.

Stay updated on the latest developments to make the most of your visit!

Chapter 1: Planning and Preparation

Best Times to Visit Universal Orlando Resort

1. January – February (Low Season): Cooler temperatures and smaller crowds. Great for shorter lines and post-holiday deals.

2. March – April (Spring Break): Warmer weather and lively atmosphere, but expect higher crowds and prices.

3. May – Early June (Pre-Summer): Lower crowds before summer peak with pleasant weather.

4. July – August (Summer Peak): Busy season with extended park hours and summer festivities. Prepare for heat and crowds.

5. September – October (Fall Season): Halloween Horror Nights (select dates) draw thrill-seekers. Lower crowds during non-event days.

6. November – December (Holiday Season): Enjoy Christmas celebrations, Grinchmas, and festive parades. Weekdays are less crowded than holidays.

For fewer crowds and comfortable weather, aim for weekdays in January, February, or September.

Website: universalorlando.com
Contact: +1-407-363-8000

Visa, Entry Requirements, and Procedures for Universal Orlando Resort

1. Visa Requirements (For International Travelers):

U.S. Citizens: No visa is required for entry into the U.S. if you are a citizen. However, you will need a valid U.S. passport for air travel.

Non-U.S. Citizens: Visa requirements vary based on nationality. Most international travelers will need a tourist visa (B-2) to enter the U.S.

2. Visa Application Process:

Visa Waiver Program (VWP): Citizens of eligible countries may enter the U.S. without a visa for stays of up to 90 days under the VWP.

Tourist Visa (B-2): If you are not eligible for the VWP, apply for a B-2 visa at a U.S. embassy or consulate in your home country. The application requires an interview, submission of documents (passport, visa application form, visa fee), and biometric data.

Cost:

B-2 Tourist Visa application fee: $160 (subject to change based on embassy requirements).

VWP: No fee, but you must apply for an ESTA (Electronic System for Travel Authorization), which costs $21.

3. Locations for Visa Application:
U.S. embassies and consulates around the world.

Find your nearest embassy or consulate: U.S. Embassy Locator

4. Entry Procedures Upon Arrival:

Complete a Customs Declaration Form and submit it to U.S. Customs and Border Protection (CBP).

Go through immigration and security checks.

If you have the necessary documents, you'll be allowed to enter the U.S. and proceed to your destination.

5. Etiquette and Customs:

Politeness: American culture values politeness and punctuality. A firm handshake is common when meeting someone for the first time.

Tipping: Tipping is customary in the U.S. for services, such as dining (15-20% of the bill), bellboys, or taxi drivers.

Public Behavior: Respect for personal space is important. Avoid loud conversations in public places.

Contacts for Further Information:

U.S. Department of State: travel.state.gov

U.S. Citizenship and Immigration Services (USCIS): uscis.gov

ESTA Application: esta.cbp.dhs.gov

Website: universalorlando.com
Contact: +1-407-363-8000

Budgeting and Packing Essentials for Universal Orlando Resort

1. Budgeting Tips:

Accommodation: Prices vary by season and proximity to the parks. On-site resorts offer perks like early park entry, but off-site hotels may be more budget-friendly. Rates range from $100 to $600+ per night depending on the type of hotel and time of year.

Tickets: A single-day park ticket starts at around $109. Consider multi-day tickets for better value. Packages with hotel stays may offer discounts.

Dining: Quick-service meals cost about $10-$15 per person, while sit-down restaurants range from $20-$50. Budget for about $50-$70 per day for food per person.

Souvenirs: Prices for park souvenirs range from $10 for small items to $100+ for collectibles or apparel. Plan to set aside $50-$100 for souvenirs, depending on your interests.

Transportation: If you're flying, budget for airport transfers (around $30-$50 each way for a taxi or shuttle). On-site hotels provide complimentary shuttle service to the parks.

2. Packing Essentials:

Clothing:

Summer (June-August): Pack lightweight, breathable clothing, sunscreen, a hat, and sunglasses. Comfortable shoes are a must for walking.

Winter (December-February): While Florida is typically mild, bring a light jacket for cooler evenings and rain gear (raincoats/umbrellas).

Fall/Spring (September-November, March-May): Layered clothing for variable temperatures. A light sweater and comfortable shoes for walking.

Park Essentials:

Water Bottle: Stay hydrated throughout the day.

Backpack or Fanny Pack: Ideal for carrying your essentials like sunscreen, snacks, and extra clothing.

Portable Charger: To keep your phone charged for photos, app use, and ticketing.

3. Weather Considerations:

Rain Gear: Florida's weather can be unpredictable, with afternoon rain showers common, especially in summer. Pack a lightweight poncho or foldable umbrella.

Comfortable Footwear: With lots of walking, comfortable, waterproof shoes are essential.

Website: universalorlando.com
Contact: +1-407-363-8000

Safety, Security, and Health Tips for Universal Orlando Resort

1. General Safety Advice:

Stay Hydrated: Florida's hot and humid weather can lead to dehydration, especially during peak summer months. Drink plenty of water throughout the day.

Use Sun Protection: Apply sunscreen regularly and wear a hat and sunglasses to protect yourself from the sun.

Follow Park Rules: Adhere to safety guidelines for rides, such as height restrictions and health warnings. Always stay alert and follow staff instructions.

Emergency Services: In case of an emergency, contact Universal Orlando Resort's security or medical teams, or dial 911 for local emergency services.

2. Health Tips:

Wear Comfortable Footwear: The parks involve a lot of walking. Ensure your shoes are well-cushioned and suitable for long hours.

Rest and Take Breaks: Take regular breaks to avoid exhaustion. The parks can be overwhelming, especially during peak seasons.

Allergies and Medications: If you have allergies or need specific medication, bring it with you. Check with the park about their policy on carrying medications in the parks.

3. Vaccinations:

Routine Vaccinations: Ensure you are up to date on standard vaccinations such as the flu shot, hepatitis A, and tetanus.

Travel Health Advice: While there are no specific vaccinations required for U.S. entry, it's always a good idea to consult with a healthcare provider before traveling for general advice based on your health condition.

COVID-19: Although policies may change, ensure you follow any local guidelines related to COVID-19 protocols, such as mask-wearing or vaccination requirements.

4. Security Tips:

Keep Valuables Safe: Use lockers for valuables when going on rides and avoid carrying large amounts of cash.

Stay in Groups: If traveling with children or a group, designate a meeting point in case anyone gets separated.

Bag Checks and Security Screening: Expect bag checks at the entrances of all parks. Only carry essential items to avoid delays.

Website: universalorlando.com
Contact: +1-407-363-8000

Language and Communication at Universal Orlando Resort

1. Primary Language:

The primary language spoken at Universal Orlando Resort is English, but you'll find a diverse range of languages spoken due to the international nature of the visitors and staff. Spanish is commonly heard, and some staff members may speak other languages such as French, German, and Portuguese.

2. Key Phrases:
While English is the primary language, here are a few key phrases that might be helpful:

Hello / Goodbye: "Hello" / "Goodbye"

Please / Thank you: "Please" / "Thank you"

Where is...?: "Where is the restroom?"

How much is this?: "How much is this?"

Excuse me: "Excuse me"

I need help: "I need help"

I don't understand: "I don't understand"

3. Language Tips:

Politeness: Americans value politeness, so using "please" and "thank you" is common and appreciated.

Clear Speech: Speak slowly and clearly. If there's a language barrier, a gentle repetition can help.

Gestures: Friendly hand gestures (like a wave or a thumbs-up) are common and easily understood.

4. Using Translation Apps:

Google Translate: A popular and free app for translating text, voice, and even images.

iTranslate: Another good option for real-time translations.

Duolingo: While it's a learning app, Duolingo can help you get basic phrases in different languages before your trip.

5. Communication at the Resort:

Universal Orlando Resort staff is accustomed to visitors from around the world. If you don't speak English fluently, they'll often try to help using simple language, and translation apps can bridge any gaps.

Website: universalorlando.com
Contact: +1-407-363-8000

Chapter 2: Sustainable and Responsible Travel

Environmental Preservation and Local Etiquette at Universal Orlando Resort

1. Environmental Preservation Tips:

Reduce, Reuse, Recycle: Universal Orlando Resort is committed to sustainability. Make use of recycling bins throughout the parks for paper, plastics, and cans. Avoid single-use plastics by carrying reusable water bottles and containers.

Energy Conservation: Be mindful of energy use in your hotel room. Turn off lights and electronics when not in use.

Respect Wildlife: Florida is home to a diverse range of wildlife. Do not disturb animals or plants, and refrain from feeding wildlife. Follow park guidelines regarding animal interactions.

Water Conservation: Be mindful of water usage, especially during the summer months when water conservation efforts are more critical. Use water sparingly and take shorter showers in the hotel.

Eco-Friendly Merchandise: Consider purchasing eco-friendly products from the park's stores, such as items made from recycled materials.

2. Local Etiquette:

Politeness and Respect: In the U.S., it's common to greet people with a handshake or a friendly "hello" and to thank people for their help. Show respect for local customs and the diverse cultural background of Orlando's population.

Trash Disposal: Always dispose of your trash properly, and if you see litter, help by picking it up. This helps keep the parks clean for everyone.

Respect the Park's Rules: Follow the park's rules and regulations, such as height restrictions for rides and safety instructions, to ensure your safety and that of others.

Behavior in Public Spaces: Keep noise levels moderate, especially in more serene areas, such as dining areas and queues. Public manners like queueing patiently are highly valued.

By being mindful of these practices, visitors can contribute to preserving the environment and maintaining a respectful atmosphere at Universal Orlando Resort.

Website: universalorlando.com
Contact: +1-407-363-8000

Travel Dos and Don'ts at Universal Orlando Resort

1. Dos:

Do Follow Park Rules: Always adhere to ride safety instructions, height requirements, and any posted guidelines. This ensures your safety and the safety of others.

Do Use Sunscreen: Florida's sun can be intense, so protect your skin by applying sunscreen frequently, especially in outdoor areas.

Do Stay Hydrated: Florida's hot climate, especially in the summer, can lead to dehydration. Carry a water bottle and refill it at the park's water fountains.

Do Use Trash Bins: Dispose of trash properly and use recycling bins for recyclable items. Keep the parks clean for all visitors.

Do Respect Queues: Wait your turn in line. Queue-jumping is considered rude and is generally not tolerated.

Do Be Polite: Greet staff and fellow visitors with respect. Saying "please" and "thank you" is appreciated.

Do Respect Personal Space: Be mindful of people's personal space, especially in crowded areas. Avoid standing too close to others.

Do Tip for Services: In the U.S., tipping is customary for services such as dining, bellhops, and shuttle drivers. A tip of 15-20% is standard in restaurants.

2. Don'ts:

Don't Disrespect the Environment: Avoid littering, damage to plants, or disturbing wildlife. Treat the natural environment with respect.

Don't Use Your Phone in Sensitive Areas: Keep your phone on silent in ride queues and indoor attractions. Avoid loud phone conversations in public areas.

Don't Skip Safety Guidelines: For your safety, do not ignore ride rules or park policies. Pay attention to warnings about height, health restrictions, and ride safety.

Don't Overpack: Avoid carrying excessive bags or heavy items. The parks involve a lot of walking, so keep your belongings minimal.

Don't Engage in Disruptive Behavior: Loud, disruptive behavior or cutting in line is frowned upon. Always be considerate of others' experiences.

Don't Take Photos in Restricted Areas: Respect areas where photography is prohibited, such as certain rides or backstage areas.

Don't Feed Animals: Avoid feeding wildlife within the park or nearby. It can be harmful to animals and is typically against park rules.

By adhering to these dos and don'ts, you'll ensure a positive experience for both yourself and those around you while respecting local customs and the park's environment.

Website: universalorlando.com
Contact: +1-407-363-8000

Minimizing Your Carbon Footprint at Universal Orlando Resort

1. Eco-Conscious Travel Options:

Public Transportation: Utilize public transportation or shared shuttle services to get to and from the park. Universal Orlando Resort offers shuttle buses and other transport options that can help reduce the number of vehicles on the road. If you're staying on-site, take advantage of the resort's complimentary transportation to minimize your carbon footprint.

Electric Vehicles (EVs): If you're driving, consider using an electric vehicle. Many hotels in the area offer EV charging stations, and Universal Orlando Resort has its own electric car charging stations for guests. This helps reduce carbon emissions from gasoline-powered vehicles.

Carpooling: If you're traveling with a group, carpool to reduce the number of cars needed for the trip. This is an effective way to lessen traffic and reduce environmental impact.

2. Eco-Friendly Practices Within the Resort:

Reusable Water Bottles: Bring a reusable water bottle to refill throughout the day. Universal Orlando Resort has water refill stations, reducing the need for single-use plastic bottles.

Sustainable Merchandise: Support the resort's efforts by purchasing eco-friendly souvenirs, such as items made from recycled materials.

Paperless Tickets: Use mobile tickets or digital passes via the Universal Orlando app to avoid printing paper tickets, helping reduce paper waste.

Recycling: Make use of the recycling bins provided throughout the parks for paper, plastic, and cans. Look for clearly marked bins and be mindful of sorting your waste properly.

3. Sustainable Accommodation Choices:

Stay at Eco-Conscious Hotels: If you're staying on-site, check for eco-friendly hotels that prioritize sustainability. Many of Universal's hotels have initiatives like energy-efficient lighting, water-saving fixtures, and a commitment to reducing plastic use.

Limit Laundry Loads: Many hotel chains, including those in the Universal Orlando Resort area, offer a towel and linen reuse program. Consider reusing towels and linens to help reduce water and energy consumption.

4. Energy Conservation:

Turn Off Lights and Electronics: In your hotel room, make sure to turn off lights, air conditioning, and electronics when you're not using them. This helps conserve energy.

Use Less Air Conditioning: Florida's warm climate means air conditioning can be tempting, but setting the thermostat higher (while still keeping things comfortable) can help save energy.

5. Support Eco-Friendly Dining:

Choose Sustainable Dining Options: Opt for restaurants that offer locally sourced ingredients or sustainable menu options. Some dining locations at Universal Orlando Resort focus on farm-to-table offerings, which can reduce the carbon footprint associated with food production and transportation.

Avoid Single-Use Plastics: Opt for meals served in sustainable packaging and avoid using disposable plastic utensils or straws when possible.

By adopting these eco-conscious travel practices, you'll help minimize your carbon footprint and contribute to a more sustainable and environmentally-friendly visit to Universal Orlando Resort.

Website: universalorlando.com
Contact: +1-407-363-8000

Avoiding Scams and Tourist Traps at Universal Orlando Resort

1. Common Scams to Watch Out For:

Ticket Scams: Only purchase tickets from official sources such as the Universal Orlando website or authorized ticket vendors. Avoid buying tickets from third-party sellers or street vendors, as they might sell counterfeit or expired tickets.

Timeshare Presentations: Some companies may offer "free" tickets or experiences in exchange for attending a timeshare presentation. These presentations are often high-pressure sales tactics. It's best to avoid engaging with such offers.

Overpriced Souvenirs: Be cautious of souvenirs sold at inflated prices outside the park or in areas surrounding the resort. Many off-site vendors target tourists with overpriced items. Always compare prices with those at Universal Orlando Resort before making a purchase.

Street Performers: While many street performers are legitimate, be wary of those who ask for money directly, especially if they put pressure on you to donate or give a "voluntary" payment for an impromptu show.

2. Avoiding Tourist Traps:

Overpriced Dining Locations: In tourist-heavy areas around the resort, there are restaurants and food stands that may charge inflated prices. Look for dining options within the park or those recommended by Universal's official website, as they typically offer better value and quality.

Excessive Souvenir Kiosks: Many kiosks around the park may sell generic souvenirs that are often overpriced. Instead, purchase items directly from Universal's official merchandise stores for authentic and better-priced souvenirs.

Themed Photo Scams: Be cautious of unofficial photographers offering to take your picture for a fee, especially in high-traffic areas near the park entrance. Universal Orlando provides official photographers for souvenir photos, and these are typically well-priced and legitimate.

3. General Tips for Staying Safe:

Stay Alert: Always be aware of your surroundings, especially when dealing with vendors or unfamiliar individuals. If someone seems overly eager or pushy, it's best to walk away.

Avoid Carrying Large Amounts of Cash: Use credit or debit cards for purchases instead of carrying large sums of cash, reducing the risk of theft. Many places at the park also accept mobile payments like Apple Pay or Google Pay.

Use the Official Universal Orlando App: The app provides official information about wait times, park maps, and attractions. It can help you navigate the resort and avoid misinformation from unreliable sources.

Ask for Help: If you're unsure about a deal or offer, don't hesitate to ask Universal Orlando staff members for advice. They can point you toward legitimate services and steer you away from potential scams.

By staying aware of these common scams and tourist traps, you can have a safe, enjoyable, and stress-free experience at Universal Orlando Resort.

Website: universalorlando.com
Contact: +1-407-363-8000

Insider Tips for Budgeting and Money Saving at Universal Orlando Resort

1. Buy Tickets in Advance:

Book Early: Purchasing tickets online ahead of time can save you both money and time. Universal Orlando often offers discounts for multi-day tickets, and buying in advance avoids the higher prices that are often charged at the gate.

Look for Special Offers: Keep an eye on special promotions or package deals offered directly through the Universal Orlando website. These can include discounts on tickets, accommodations, or dining plans.

2. Stay at On-Site Hotels for Added Benefits:

Stay at Value Hotels: Universal Orlando Resort has budget-friendly hotel options like Universal's Endless Summer Resort – Dockside Inn and Suites. Staying on-site can save you money on parking, and you'll also get early park access, helping you maximize your time in the parks.

Free Shuttle Service: Most on-site hotels offer free shuttle transportation to the parks, which saves on parking fees (which can be $25 per day).

Take Advantage of Hotel Perks: Many of Universal's hotels include perks like early park entry, free Wi-Fi, and dining discounts. These benefits can offset the cost of accommodation.

3. Bring Your Own Snacks and Water:

Avoid Overpriced Food: Food and drink at Universal Orlando Resort can be expensive. You're allowed to bring in your own snacks and refillable water bottle, which can save you money throughout the day. Some parks even have free water refill stations.

Pack a Picnic: If you're planning to spend the whole day in the parks, consider packing a lunch. Many guests pack sandwiches or snacks to enjoy during breaks in the park, reducing the need to purchase pricey meals.

4. Use the Universal Orlando App:

Track Dining and Shopping Deals: The Universal Orlando app provides information about in-park discounts and meal options. You can find meal deals, including combo meals, and make reservations for table service restaurants.

Plan Your Meals Around Off-Peak Times: Dining at less busy times, like early lunch or late dinner, can save you money. You'll avoid peak pricing and long wait times.

5. Consider a Dining Plan:

Universal Dining Plans: If you plan on eating in the park frequently, consider purchasing a dining plan. The Universal Dining Plan offers an all-inclusive approach to food and beverage, which can save you money if you plan to eat at sit-down restaurants.

Opt for Quick-Service Meals: For more budget-friendly options, stick to quick-service eateries where you can find meals under $10, like pizza, salads, or burgers.

6. Set a Daily Budget:

Track Spending: Before your trip, set a daily budget for food, souvenirs, and additional expenses like photos or special experiences. Stick to this budget by using cash or a prepaid card, which helps you avoid overspending.

Look for Free or Low-Cost Activities: While Universal Orlando Resort is known for its attractions, there are also free or low-cost activities available, like character meet-and-greets, parades, and street performances. These can be fun without adding to your expenses.

7. Avoid Souvenir Overload:

Set a Souvenir Budget: The parks are full of tempting souvenirs, but they can add up quickly. Set a specific budget for souvenirs and stick to it. Consider purchasing a Universal Orlando Resort souvenir cup, which offers unlimited refills at participating locations during your stay.

Buy Souvenirs Online: Universal's online store often has discounted merchandise, so you might be able to find a souvenir you want without paying full price at the park.

By implementing these insider tips, you can enjoy Universal Orlando Resort without breaking the bank while still making the most of your visit.

Website: universalorlando.com
Contact: +1-407-363-8000

Chapter 3: Getting Around and Navigating Universal Orlando Resort

Arriving and Departing Universal Orlando Resort

1. Airports Near Universal Orlando Resort:

Orlando International Airport (MCO):
This is the primary airport for travelers heading to Universal Orlando Resort. Located about 12 miles (20 km) southeast of the resort, it's the most convenient option for international and domestic flights. The airport is well-served by taxis, shuttles, and rental cars.

Distance to Universal Orlando Resort: Approximately 20 minutes by car.

Website: orlandoairports.net

Contact: +1-407-825-2001

Orlando Sanford International Airport (SFB):
Located about 30 miles (48 km) from Universal Orlando Resort, this airport is a secondary option, mainly serving charter flights and low-cost carriers.

Distance to Universal Orlando Resort: Approximately 45 minutes by car.

Website: orlandoairports.net

Contact: +1-407-585-4000

2. Public Transport Options:

Shuttle Services:
Universal Orlando Resort offers complimentary shuttle transportation for guests staying at their on-site hotels. This service connects directly from Orlando International Airport to the Universal hotels. Additionally, many third-party shuttle services operate from both Orlando International and Sanford International airports to Universal Orlando.

Cost: Typically ranges from $20 to $35 per person for one-way service.

Booking: Contact your hotel or visit third-party shuttle services like Mears Transportation for reservations.

Public Buses:

Lynx Bus Service: The Lynx public bus system operates throughout Orlando and has routes connecting the airport to various parts of the city, including stops near Universal Orlando Resort.

Bus Stop at MCO: Buses depart regularly from the airport to different areas of Orlando, including Universal Orlando.

Cost: $2 per ride for a single ticket.

Website: golynx.com

Contact: +1-407-841-5969

Taxis and Ride-Sharing Services:

Taxis: Available at designated taxi stands outside both airport terminals. A taxi ride from Orlando International Airport to Universal Orlando Resort typically costs between $35 to $50.

Ride-Sharing: Services like Uber and Lyft are widely available at both airports and can be a more cost-effective alternative.

Cost: Uber/Lyft fares range from $20 to $40 depending on the time of day and type of service selected.

3. Navigating the Resort:

On-Site Shuttle Services: If you are staying at a Universal Orlando Resort hotel, free shuttles are available to take you directly to the parks. These shuttles also operate between the parks and CityWalk.

Walking: Many on-site hotels are within walking distance of the parks, especially those in the Universal Studios area.

Parking: If you're driving, Universal Orlando Resort offers parking at its various locations, including the parks and CityWalk. Expect to pay between $25 to $30 for daily parking. Valet parking is also available for higher fees.

4. Departing Universal Orlando Resort:

Hotel Shuttles: If you're staying at a Universal Orlando Resort hotel, your shuttle will take you back to the airport. Make sure to confirm departure times with the hotel front desk ahead of time.

Taxis and Ride-Sharing: Taxis and ride-sharing services are also available for transportation back to the airport. Be sure to request your ride well in advance to avoid delays.

Public Transport: For budget-conscious travelers, Lynx buses can be a convenient and affordable way to get back to Orlando International Airport.

Website for Transportation Services:

Mears Transportation

Universal Orlando Resort
Contact: +1-407-363-8000

Local Transportation Options for Universal Orlando Resort

1. Buses (Lynx Public Transit):

Description: Lynx is Orlando's public bus system, offering affordable transportation throughout the city, including stops near Universal Orlando Resort. It's an economical choice for travelers on a budget.

Locations: Buses run between major tourist areas, including stops near Orlando International Airport (MCO), Universal Orlando Resort, and Downtown Orlando.

Costs: A single ride costs $2.00. Multi-ride passes are available at a discounted rate, with a 7-day pass priced around $16.50.

Etiquette: Always have the exact fare, as drivers don't give change. Be respectful of other passengers and keep your volume low.

Contact: +1-407-841-5969

Website: golynx.com

2. Taxis:

Description: Taxis are readily available at Universal Orlando Resort and nearby locations like Orlando International Airport (MCO). They provide direct, door-to-door service and are a good option for travelers who prefer convenience.

Locations: Taxi stands are located at Universal Orlando Resort hotels and at the airport. Taxis can also be hailed directly from the street or through dispatch services.

Costs: A taxi ride from Orlando International Airport (MCO) to Universal Orlando Resort costs around $35-$50, depending on traffic and time of day. Short trips within the resort area may cost $10-$15.

Etiquette: Be respectful and polite to the driver. Tipping 10-15% is standard.

Contact: Yellow Taxi - +1-407-699-9999

Website: orlandotaxi.com

3. Ride-Sharing Services (Uber & Lyft):

Description: Uber and Lyft are popular ride-sharing services in Orlando, providing a more affordable and flexible alternative to taxis. Both services can be easily accessed via their respective mobile apps.

Locations: Pick-up and drop-off points are available at Universal Orlando Resort, including at designated areas for Uber/Lyft riders.

Costs: Prices for a ride from Orlando International Airport (MCO) to Universal Orlando Resort typically range from $20-$40, depending on factors like ride type and demand.

Etiquette: Always confirm your ride through the app before entering the vehicle. Follow the driver's instructions for pick-up locations, especially at crowded spots.

Contact:

Uber: +1-800-593-7069

Lyft: +1-844-250-2773

Websites:

Uber

Lyft

4. Car Rentals:

Description: Renting a car gives you the flexibility to explore Orlando and surrounding areas at your own pace. There are several car rental agencies near Universal Orlando Resort and Orlando International Airport.

Locations: Major car rental agencies like Enterprise, Hertz, Avis, and Budget are available at Orlando International Airport (MCO), and some offer pick-up/drop-off services at nearby hotels.

Costs: Rental car prices vary based on the vehicle type, with rates typically starting around $30-$50 per day for an economy car.

Etiquette: Be mindful of parking fees at Universal Orlando Resort (typically $25-$30 per day), and always return the vehicle on time to avoid extra charges.

Contact:

Enterprise: +1-407-827-2700

Hertz: +1-407-855-2121

Avis: +1-407-856-1110

Budget: +1-800-218-7992

Websites:

Enterprise

Hertz

Avis

Budget

5. Cycling Options:

Description: Orlando is becoming increasingly bike-friendly, with many bike lanes and paths throughout the city. However, bike rentals are not as common within Universal Orlando Resort itself.

Locations: Several nearby neighborhoods and hotels may offer bicycle rentals. For example, the Bike Share Program provides access to bikes at various locations throughout the city.

Costs: Bike rentals typically cost around $10-$20 per day, depending on the service provider and the type of bike.

Etiquette: Always wear a helmet (available for rent in some places), follow traffic rules, and be considerate of pedestrians when biking near Universal Orlando Resort.

Contact:

LimeBike

Jump Bikes

Website: Orlando Bike Share

By using these local transportation options, you can efficiently and affordably navigate Universal Orlando Resort and the surrounding areas. Whether you prefer the convenience of taxis or the flexibility of car rentals, there are options available to suit every traveler's needs.

Transportation Tips for Universal Orlando Resort

1. Use Apps for Easy Navigation and Ticket Booking:

Google Maps: It's a must-have for navigating Orlando, whether you're walking, driving, or using public transport. It provides real-time updates on bus routes, ride-sharing options, and even walking directions to Universal Orlando Resort.

Tip: Always check for traffic updates when traveling by car or taxi to avoid delays.

LYNX Bus Tracker: For those using Orlando's public buses, the LYNX app allows you to track bus routes in real-time and provides schedules and fares.

Download: Available on both iOS and Android.

Tip: Use the app to see when the next bus is arriving so you don't have to wait outside unnecessarily.

Uber & Lyft: These ride-sharing apps are incredibly convenient and user-friendly. You can easily book a ride from your phone to and from Universal Orlando Resort or anywhere in Orlando. Both apps also show estimated fares and wait times.

Tip: If traveling during peak hours, consider choosing a larger vehicle like an UberXL to avoid surcharges from surge pricing.

2. Smart Use of Public Transport:

Use the Exact Fare on Buses: If you're taking a Lynx bus, make sure you have the exact fare ready, as drivers cannot provide change. Consider purchasing a bus pass for multiple rides if you're staying in Orlando for an extended period.

Tip: Buy a 7-day pass ($16.50) for convenience and savings if you plan to use the bus multiple times.

Plan Your Route in Advance: Use the Google Maps or Lynx app to plan your journey ahead of time. It will provide all available transportation options and the quickest routes to your destination.

Tip: Always check departure times, especially if you're headed to the park early or late, as bus schedules may vary during holidays or weekends.

3. Choosing the Right Taxi or Ride-Share Service:

Uber & Lyft Over Taxis: While taxis are available, ride-sharing services like Uber and Lyft tend to be more cost-effective and flexible. They also have less waiting time since you can track your ride in real time.

Tip: Use UberPool or Lyft Line for shared rides to save money, though this may increase your travel time slightly.

Pick-up and Drop-off Locations: Uber and Lyft drivers at Universal Orlando Resort have designated pick-up/drop-off spots. These spots are usually near the entrance, but be sure to check in the app for the exact location.

Tip: During peak times, pick-up areas may get crowded, so plan for extra time when requesting a ride.

4. Car Rental Tips:

Use a GPS or Navigation App: Orlando's roads can be busy and confusing for first-time visitors, so using a navigation app like Google Maps or Waze can help you avoid traffic and find the quickest routes to and from Universal Orlando Resort.

Tip: If you're renting a car, avoid driving during rush hour (8-9 AM and 4-6 PM) when traffic is heaviest. Parking fees at Universal Orlando Resort are around $25 to $30 per day.

Book Car Rentals in Advance: If you need a car, book it online before you arrive to ensure availability, especially during peak seasons. Popular rental companies like Hertz, Enterprise, and Budget are located at Orlando International Airport.

Tip: Look for deals on car rental sites or apps like Kayak or Expedia for discounted rates.

5. Bicycle Rentals:

Bike Share Programs: If you prefer cycling, Orlando's bike-sharing program (LimeBike, Jump Bikes) allows you to rent bikes easily through the app. Simply unlock the bike with your smartphone and start cycling around.

Tip: Remember to check the bike for any damage before starting, and always wear a helmet for safety.

6. General Travel Hacks:

Download the Universal Orlando Resort App: This app offers real-time information about park hours, wait times, directions to various attractions, and available transport options within the resort.

Parking Hacks: If you're driving and planning to visit multiple parks in one day, look for the "Preferred Parking" spots for closer proximity to the park entrances, though they are slightly more expensive.

Tip: If you're staying at one of Universal Orlando's on-site hotels, take advantage of the free shuttle services instead of driving to avoid parking fees.

By utilizing apps for navigation and ticket booking, and following these practical transportation tips, you can make your travel to and from Universal Orlando Resort as seamless and stress-free as possible.

Maps and Navigation Tools for Universal Orlando Resort

1. Google Maps:

Description: Google Maps is the most widely used navigation app, providing detailed directions for driving, walking, and public transportation. It offers real-time updates, estimated arrival times, and accurate directions.

Features:

Step-by-step navigation for driving, walking, and public transport.

Real-time traffic updates.

Street view to help visualize locations.

Details on restaurants, shops, and attractions near Universal Orlando Resort.

Link: Google Maps

Tip: Use Google Maps for both getting to Universal Orlando Resort and navigating within the resort for attractions, dining, and parking.

2. Universal Orlando Resort Official App:

Description: The official Universal Orlando Resort app provides detailed maps and live updates for the theme parks. It helps you navigate the park, check wait times, find showtimes, and even make dining reservations.

Features:

Interactive maps of Universal Studios Florida, Islands of Adventure, and Universal CityWalk.

Real-time wait times for rides and attractions.

Show schedules and dining options.

Ability to purchase tickets and make reservations directly through the app.

Link: Universal Orlando Resort App

Tip: Download this app to avoid getting lost in the resort and stay updated on everything happening inside.

3. Lynx Bus Tracker:

Description: If you're using public transportation to get around Orlando, the Lynx Bus Tracker app is a useful tool. It provides real-time tracking of bus routes and schedules for the city's public bus system.

Features:

Live tracking of bus routes in Orlando.

Updates on arrival times for buses at specific stops.

Route planning based on your destination.

Link: Lynx Bus Tracker App

Tip: Use this app to plan your public transport routes and ensure you catch the right bus to Universal Orlando Resort.

4. Waze:

Description: Waze is a community-driven navigation app that provides real-time traffic updates, road hazards, and optimal driving routes based on input from users.

Features:

Real-time traffic alerts and route adjustments.

Alerts about accidents, road closures, and hazards.

Fastest route suggestions based on current conditions.

Link: Waze

Tip: Waze is ideal for travelers driving to Universal Orlando Resort to avoid traffic jams and optimize travel time.

5. Apple Maps:

Description: Apple Maps is the default navigation app for iPhone users, providing turn-by-turn directions and real-time traffic information. It also integrates with other Apple services, like Siri and the Apple Watch.

Features:

Turn-by-turn directions for driving, walking, and public transport.

Real-time traffic conditions and suggested routes.

Detailed information about points of interest, including attractions, restaurants, and hotels near Universal Orlando Resort.

Link: Apple Maps

Tip: Apple Maps is a great alternative for iPhone users, with up-to-date traffic and route information.

6. Citymapper:

Description: Citymapper is an excellent app for navigating cities with public transport systems. It combines data from buses, trains, subways, and walking to suggest the best routes in Orlando.

Features:

Public transport routes, times, and connections.

Walking directions and bike routes.

Integration with ride-sharing services like Uber and Lyft.

Link: Citymapper

Tip: Use Citymapper for public transit, particularly if you are exploring Orlando and need to navigate various modes of transportation.

7. Map of Universal Orlando Resort (Printed and Digital):

Description: A detailed map of the Universal Orlando Resort is available in both printed and digital formats. It provides information on park layouts, rides, dining, shops, and other attractions.

Features:

Interactive digital map available on the Universal Orlando Resort website and app.

Printed maps available at the park entrance.

Link: Universal Orlando Resort Map

Tip: Grab a printed map when you enter the park or refer to the digital version for easy access to essential information during your visit.

These tools will help you navigate Universal Orlando Resort and the greater Orlando area efficiently, ensuring you spend more time enjoying the attractions and less time lost. Whether you're using public transport or driving, these apps and maps will help you find your way with ease.

Chapter 4: Where to Stay

Accommodation Options by Budget for Universal Orlando Resort

1. Budget Accommodation

Location: Near Universal Orlando Resort or off-site in the broader Orlando area.

Average Cost: $50 - $100 per night

Options:

Quality Inn & Suites (Near Universal Orlando Resort)

Description: Affordable, no-frills hotel offering complimentary breakfast and free shuttle service to Universal Orlando Resort.

Cost: Around $80-$100 per night.

Contact: +1 (407) 351-2121

Website: Quality Inn

Tip: Ideal for travelers who prioritize saving money while still being close to the park. Early booking is recommended to get the best rates.

Econo Lodge (Near Universal Studios)

Description: Budget-friendly with basic amenities, offering free parking and shuttle to Universal.

Cost: Around $60-$80 per night.

Contact: +1 (407) 351-6200

Website: Econo Lodge

Tip: Great option for those looking for a simple, no-frills stay near Universal Orlando Resort.

2. Mid-Range Accommodation

Location: On-site at Universal Orlando Resort or within a short drive.

Average Cost: $100 - $250 per night

Options:

Universal's Cabana Bay Beach Resort

Description: A retro-style resort with a laid-back vibe, offering modern amenities, multiple pools, and dining options. Free shuttle service to Universal parks.

Cost: Around $150-$250 per night.

Contact: +1 (888) 273-1311

Website: Cabana Bay Beach Resort

Tip: Offers excellent value for those looking for on-site accommodation with themed atmospheres. Book early for discounts.

Holiday Inn & Suites Across from Universal Orlando

Description: A family-friendly hotel with spacious rooms, a pool, and free shuttle service to the Universal parks.

Cost: Around $120-$190 per night.

Contact: +1 (407) 351-3333

Website: Holiday Inn & Suites

Tip: Ideal for families looking for a comfortable stay near the parks with all the necessary amenities.

3. Luxury Accommodation

Location: On-site at Universal Orlando Resort, close to the parks.

Average Cost: $250 - $500+ per night

Options:

Hard Rock Hotel® at Universal Orlando

Description: A luxury hotel offering exclusive perks like Early Park Admission, upscale dining, and a rock-n-roll theme. Walking distance to Universal Studios Florida.

Cost: Around $350-$500+ per night.

Contact: +1 (888) 464-3617

Website: Hard Rock Hotel Orlando

Tip: The perfect choice for luxury seekers, with access to exclusive events and VIP treatment at Universal parks.

Loews Sapphire Falls Resort at Universal Orlando

Description: A tropical escape with a large lagoon-style pool, unique dining experiences, and free shuttle service to Universal Orlando Resort.

Cost: Around $250-$400 per night.

Contact: +1 (888) 273-1311

Website: Sapphire Falls Resort

Tip: This resort offers a relaxing atmosphere and unique Caribbean-inspired décor, perfect for those looking for a more immersive experience.

4. Luxury Vacation Rentals

Location: Nearby areas such as International Drive, Lake Buena Vista, and Celebration.

Average Cost: $150 - $500+ per night (depending on size and amenities)

Options:

Airbnb & VRBO: Luxury vacation homes, condos, and apartments near Universal Orlando Resort.

Description: Choose from a wide variety of luxury vacation homes or condos, offering full kitchens, pools, and private spaces for families and large groups.

Cost: Varies, typically $150 to $500+ per night, depending on size and amenities.

Contact: Visit Airbnb or VRBO websites for property contacts and booking.

Website: Airbnb | VRBO

Tip: Great for groups or families who prefer more space and the flexibility of self-catering. Ensure to check reviews and property amenities for a seamless experience.

5. Etiquette Tips:

Booking Early: For both budget and luxury stays, booking in advance can help you secure the best rates, especially during peak seasons like holidays and summer.

Tipping: It's common practice to tip hotel staff, including bellhops and housekeepers, around $1-$2 per service. For concierge or valet services, a tip of $5-$10 is appreciated.

Respectful Behavior: If staying at a resort with shared spaces like pools or dining areas, be mindful of noise levels, especially in common areas. Keep noise to a respectful level after 10 PM.

With options for every budget, from affordable motels to luxurious on-site resorts, Universal Orlando Resort offers accommodations that cater to all types of travelers. Whether you're looking for basic amenities or an upscale experience, you'll find something that suits your needs. Always consider the proximity to the parks, the amenities offered, and any special perks like early park access or free shuttle services when making your choice.

Neighborhood Guides for Universal Orlando Resort

1. International Drive (I-Drive)

Description: International Drive is a bustling, vibrant area in Orlando, known for its wide variety of hotels, restaurants, and entertainment options. It's just a short drive from Universal Orlando Resort, making it a prime location for visitors who want easy access to the theme parks while being in the heart of Orlando's entertainment district.

Popular Lodging Options:

Budget:

Econo Lodge International Drive – Affordable rooms with basic amenities, close to shopping and dining.

Contact: +1 (407) 351-6200

Website: Econo Lodge

Mid-Range:

Rosen Inn at Pointe Orlando – Family-friendly hotel offering a shuttle to Universal, outdoor pool, and on-site dining.

Contact: +1 (407) 996-8585

Website: Rosen Inn

Luxury:

Wyndham Orlando Resort International Drive – A spacious resort with pools, dining options, and a close proximity to Universal.

Contact: +1 (407) 351-2420

Website: Wyndham Orlando Resort

Neighborhood Features:

Shopping: Pointe Orlando, ICON Park, and nearby outlets.

Dining: Numerous restaurants offering international cuisine, fast food, and upscale dining.

Attractions: The Wheel at ICON Park, Sea Life Orlando Aquarium, Madame Tussauds.

2. Universal CityWalk Area (On-Site Resort Area)

Description: Universal CityWalk is not just a dining and entertainment hub; it's also home to several high-end and themed accommodations. Staying in or near CityWalk offers the ultimate convenience, with walking access to Universal Studios Florida, Islands of Adventure, and Volcano Bay.

Popular Lodging Options:

Luxury:

Hard Rock Hotel® at Universal Orlando – A luxury resort with rock-and-roll themes, exclusive perks like Early Park Admission, and premium service.

Contact: +1 (888) 464-3617

Website: Hard Rock Hotel Orlando

Mid-Range:

Loews Sapphire Falls Resort at Universal Orlando – A Caribbean-inspired resort with easy access to CityWalk and Universal parks, offering a tropical escape.

Contact: +1 (888) 273-1311

Website: Sapphire Falls Resort

Budget:

Universal's Endless Summer Resort - Dockside Inn and Suites – Affordable, family-friendly accommodation with a beach-themed atmosphere and shuttle access to the parks.

Contact: +1 (888) 273-1311

Website: Endless Summer Resort

Neighborhood Features:

Entertainment: Universal CityWalk offers an array of dining options, live music, and nightlife.

Dining: Restaurants like the Hard Rock Café, Jimmy Buffett's Margaritaville, and the Toothsome Chocolate Emporium & Savory Feast Kitchen.

Shopping: Unique shops, themed merchandise, and gifts from Universal Studios.

3. Lake Buena Vista

Description: Located just outside of Disney World and close to Universal Orlando Resort, Lake Buena Vista offers a peaceful, suburban feel with quick access to both theme parks. It's perfect for families or travelers looking for a quiet place to stay but still within reach of Orlando's major attractions.

Popular Lodging Options:

Mid-Range:

Holiday Inn Orlando – Disney Springs® Area – A comfortable, family-friendly hotel with shuttle services to both Universal and Disney parks.

Contact: +1 (407) 828-8888

Website: Holiday Inn Disney Springs

Luxury:

Four Seasons Resort Orlando at Walt Disney World® Resort – Luxury accommodations with exclusive park perks, world-class dining, and a golf course.

Contact: +1 (407) 313-7777

Website: Four Seasons Resort

Budget:

Best Western Lake Buena Vista – Disney Springs® Resort Area – A budget-friendly option with a convenient location and free shuttle to the theme parks.

Contact: +1 (407) 827-1100

Website: Best Western Lake Buena Vista

Neighborhood Features:

Shopping: Disney Springs, a major shopping, dining, and entertainment district.

Dining: Numerous family-friendly restaurants with everything from fast food to gourmet options.

Attractions: Disney Springs, golf courses, and easy access to both Universal and Disney theme parks.

4. Kissimmee

Description: A bit farther from Universal Orlando Resort but still an affordable option, Kissimmee offers a range of lodging from budget motels to vacation rentals. It's a good base for families looking for more affordable accommodations while still being within a short drive of Orlando's top attractions.

Popular Lodging Options:

Budget:

Super 8 by Wyndham Kissimmee – A budget motel with free breakfast, Wi-Fi, and close proximity to the theme parks.

Contact: +1 (407) 396-0000

Website: Super 8 Kissimmee

Mid-Range:

Comfort Suites Maingate East – Located in Kissimmee with free shuttle service to Universal Orlando Resort.

Contact: +1 (407) 396-4000

Website: Comfort Suites Maingate East

Luxury:

Margaritaville Resort Orlando – A resort-style property with luxurious cottages and suites, a large pool, and exclusive amenities.

Contact: +1 (888) 717-4953

Website: Margaritaville Resort

Neighborhood Features:

Shopping: Osceola Square Mall, Kissimmee's Old Town, and many outlet stores.

Dining: International and American restaurants, fast food, and themed eateries.

Attractions: Old Town, Gatorland, and access to the Central Florida Greenway (SR 417) for easy access to other attractions.

Family-Friendly Accommodations Near Universal Orlando Resort

1. Universal's Cabana Bay Beach Resort

Location: 6550 Adventure Way, Orlando, FL 32819

Description: A retro-themed resort offering spacious family suites and standard rooms. Perfect for families who want to stay close to the parks while enjoying fun amenities like a lazy river pool, bowling alley, and interactive game rooms.

Costs: Rooms start at approximately $130–$220 per night, depending on the season.

Contact: +1 (888) 273-1311

Website: Cabana Bay Beach Resort

Etiquette: Families with young children are encouraged to enjoy the pool areas and common spaces, but noise levels should be kept respectful in hallways to avoid disturbing other guests. Expect family-friendly dining options.

2. Wyndham Orlando Resort International Drive

Location: 8001 International Drive, Orlando, FL 32819

Description: A family-oriented resort just a short drive from Universal Orlando Resort. The hotel offers family suites, kid-friendly pools, and a variety of recreational activities, including a children's play area.

Costs: Rooms start around $100–$170 per night.

Contact: +1 (407) 351-2420

Website: Wyndham Orlando Resort

Etiquette: Families are encouraged to make use of the spacious outdoor areas, including the gardens and pool, and enjoy the on-site dining facilities. Remember to maintain a friendly attitude in public spaces, especially in communal areas like the pool.

3. Loews Sapphire Falls Resort at Universal Orlando

Location: 6601 Adventure Way, Orlando, FL 32819

Description: This Caribbean-inspired resort offers spacious rooms and family suites, as well as on-site dining options and water taxis that transport guests directly to Universal Studios. It's ideal for families who want convenience and a relaxed, tropical setting.

Costs: Rates typically range from $210–$300 per night.

Contact: +1 (888) 273-1311

Website: Loews Sapphire Falls Resort

Etiquette: Families with children are invited to use the family-friendly pools and recreational areas. It's important to keep children supervised in the pools and public spaces. The staff will often accommodate families by offering early check-in or late check-out, when possible.

4. Holiday Inn Resort Orlando Suites – Waterpark

Location: 14500 Continental Gateway, Orlando, FL 32821

Description: This resort features family suites with kitchenettes and a large waterpark that kids will love, along with various kid-friendly activities and amenities. It's a bit farther from Universal Orlando but offers great family-centric experiences.

Costs: Rooms start at approximately $110–$160 per night.

Contact: +1 (407) 387-5437

Website: Holiday Inn Resort Orlando Suites

Etiquette: With a waterpark on-site, it's ideal for families with children. Parents should supervise their kids at all times, especially in the pool areas. The resort's family activities are great for entertainment during downtime.

5. Great Wolf Lodge Orlando

Location: 1400 E Buena Vista Dr, Orlando, FL 32830

Description: This resort is perfect for families looking for an all-inclusive, action-packed experience. Great Wolf Lodge features an indoor water park, themed suites, character experiences, and multiple dining options for kids of all ages.

Costs: Prices range from $180–$400 per night, depending on the type of suite and the season.

Contact: +1 (407) 919-3600

Website: Great Wolf Lodge Orlando

Etiquette: The hotel is very family-centric, so noise levels can be high, but guests should always be mindful of quiet hours, especially in hallways or when using elevators. The hotel offers various themed activities, so be respectful of staff-led programs and group experiences.

6. The Point Hotel & Suites

Location: 7389 Universal Blvd, Orlando, FL 32819

Description: Located just a short distance from Universal Orlando Resort, The Point Hotel & Suites offers spacious suites with kitchenettes, perfect for families. The resort has a heated outdoor pool and offers a free shuttle to Universal Studios.

Costs: Rates start at about $120–$190 per night.

Contact: +1 (407) 351-2400

Website: The Point Hotel & Suites

Etiquette: Families are welcome to use the outdoor pool, but children should be supervised at all times. Since the resort caters to both families and business travelers, being considerate of others' need for quietness in common areas is appreciated.

7. Drury Inn & Suites Orlando

Location: 7301 West Sand Lake Road, Orlando, FL 32819

Description: Located near Universal Orlando Resort, Drury Inn offers complimentary breakfast and evening snacks, perfect for families who need a quick bite before or after their park visits. It also has family suites, a pool, and an arcade.

Costs: Starting at $125–$180 per night.

Contact: +1 (407) 355-1100

Website: Drury Inn & Suites

Etiquette: Guests should respect others' meal times during the complimentary breakfast and evening reception. As a family-friendly hotel, it's important to be mindful of noise levels, particularly around the pool area.

8. The Hilton Orlando Bonnet Creek

Location: 14100 Bonnet Creek Resort Lane, Orlando, FL 32821

Description: Located near Disney World, but with convenient access to Universal Orlando Resort, the Hilton offers spacious family rooms, a lazy river pool, and family-friendly dining options.

Costs: Rates start at approximately $200–$350 per night.

Contact: +1 (407) 597-3600

Website: Hilton Orlando Bonnet Creek

Etiquette: Families with children are encouraged to enjoy the pool and spacious outdoor areas. Be respectful of pool hours and common areas, as the hotel also caters to business travelers.

9. Fairfield Inn & Suites by Marriott Orlando

Location: 5614 Vineland Road, Orlando, FL 32819

Description: Offering family suites and a convenient location just minutes away from Universal Orlando Resort, Fairfield Inn is ideal for families who want a balance of affordability and comfort. The hotel features a family-friendly atmosphere with a heated pool and free breakfast.

Costs: Rates start at around $120–$180 per night.

Contact: +1 (407) 351-7373

Website: Fairfield Inn & Suites

Etiquette: As this hotel caters to families, it's important to maintain courteous behavior in public spaces, including during breakfast hours and around the pool.

Inclusive and LGBTQ+ Friendly Stays Near Universal Orlando Resort

Here's a list of LGBTQ+ friendly accommodations near Universal Orlando Resort, offering inclusive environments where all guests feel welcome and respected:

1. The Grove Resort & Water Park Orlando

Location: 14501 Grove Resort Ave, Winter Garden, FL 34787

Description: An LGBTQ+-friendly resort that promotes inclusivity with welcoming policies for all. The Grove features spacious suites, a water park, and multiple dining options. Its relaxed and accepting atmosphere makes it ideal for LGBTQ+ travelers looking for a family-friendly yet inclusive stay.

Costs: Starting at $150–$250 per night.

Contact: +1 (407) 545-7500

Website: The Grove Resort

Etiquette: Respect is a core value here, ensuring a safe and comfortable environment for LGBTQ+ guests. Guests should respect the shared spaces, particularly by maintaining a family-friendly atmosphere by the pool and common areas.

2. Loews Sapphire Falls Resort at Universal Orlando

Location: 6601 Adventure Way, Orlando, FL 32819

Description: Loews Sapphire Falls Resort is known for its commitment to inclusivity and LGBTQ+ equality. The resort offers luxurious accommodations, Caribbean-inspired rooms, water taxis, and multiple dining options. Universal Orlando's own commitment to diversity ensures a welcoming atmosphere for all.

Costs: Rates typically range from $210–$300 per night.

Contact: +1 (888) 273-1311

Website: Loews Sapphire Falls Resort

Etiquette: Loews Resorts have a longstanding commitment to equality and LGBTQ+ rights. Respectful behavior in common areas is encouraged, and guests can expect warm, welcoming service from staff who are trained to ensure all guests feel at home.

3. Wyndham Orlando Resort International Drive

Location: 8001 International Drive, Orlando, FL 32819

Description: This resort prides itself on being inclusive and LGBTQ+ friendly, offering a comfortable environment for guests of all orientations. The Wyndham features family suites, pools, a fitness center, and close proximity to the Universal theme parks.

Costs: Rooms start at approximately $100–$170 per night.

Contact: +1 (407) 351-2420

Website: Wyndham Orlando Resort

Etiquette: Guests are encouraged to enjoy the facilities with respect and understanding of all backgrounds. As a family-oriented hotel, LGBTQ+ visitors will find a safe, non-judgmental environment in which to relax and enjoy their stay.

4. The Point Hotel & Suites

Location: 7389 Universal Blvd, Orlando, FL 32819

Description: The Point Hotel & Suites is recognized for offering an inclusive atmosphere, catering to the needs of LGBTQ+ travelers with excellent service and amenities. Located just minutes away from Universal Orlando Resort, it offers spacious suites and family-friendly options.

Costs: Rates start at about $120–$190 per night.

Contact: +1 (407) 351-2400

Website: The Point Hotel & Suites

Etiquette: Respect for diverse cultures and identities is encouraged. The hotel staff maintains a welcoming and inclusive attitude toward all guests, ensuring a positive experience for LGBTQ+ travelers. Keeping noise levels down in shared spaces is important for everyone's comfort.

5. Drury Inn & Suites Orlando

Location: 7301 West Sand Lake Road, Orlando, FL 32819

Description: Drury Inn is an LGBTQ+ friendly hotel offering modern amenities, free breakfast, and an evening social hour. The hotel is just a short distance from Universal Orlando Resort and offers a warm, inclusive environment.

Costs: Rates start at around $125–$180 per night.

Contact: +1 (407) 355-1100

Website: Drury Inn & Suites

Etiquette: Drury Hotels pride themselves on inclusivity, ensuring a safe space for LGBTQ+ guests. Visitors should be mindful of common area etiquette, particularly during meal times and public social hours. Respecting personal space and maintaining quiet in hallways is essential.

6. Hard Rock Hotel at Universal Orlando

Location: 5800 Universal Blvd, Orlando, FL 32819

Description: A vibrant, inclusive hotel within Universal Orlando Resort that offers a rock-star experience for all guests, regardless of sexual orientation or gender identity. The Hard Rock Hotel is known for its welcoming atmosphere and LGBTQ+ friendly policies.

Costs: Rates typically range from $250–$450 per night.

Contact: +1 (888) 423-4653

Website: Hard Rock Hotel

Etiquette: The Hard Rock Hotel's staff is trained to respect diversity and promote inclusivity. Guests are encouraged to respect the shared spaces, such as the pool area and entertainment spaces, and keep noise to a minimum in hallways.

7. Hilton Orlando Bonnet Creek

Location: 14100 Bonnet Creek Resort Lane, Orlando, FL 32821

Description: This luxurious resort offers a safe and inclusive space for LGBTQ+ guests, with spacious rooms, outdoor pools, and exceptional customer service. Located near Walt Disney World Resort, Hilton Orlando Bonnet Creek provides an ideal location for both LGBTQ+ and general travelers.

Costs: Rates start at approximately $200–$350 per night.

Contact: +1 (407) 597-3600

Website: Hilton Orlando Bonnet Creek

Etiquette: Guests are encouraged to use the spa, pools, and other amenities respectfully. The hotel's diverse and accepting atmosphere ensures all guests feel welcome, and visitors should follow hotel policies to maintain a peaceful environment.

8. Loews Royal Pacific Resort at Universal Orlando

Location: 6300 Hollywood Way, Orlando, FL 32819

Description: Another inclusive and LGBTQ+ friendly option within the Universal Orlando Resort, Loews Royal Pacific offers a relaxed, tropical atmosphere with luxury amenities, water taxis, and access to Universal Studios. The resort is part of Universal's commitment to inclusivity and offers a diverse, welcoming experience.

Costs: Rates range from $200–$350 per night.

Contact: +1 (888) 273-1311

Website: Loews Royal Pacific Resort

Etiquette: As with all Loews hotels, respect and inclusivity are key components of the guest experience. Keeping noise levels down and maintaining respectful behavior in public spaces is expected.

9. Econo Lodge International Drive

Location: 7102 International Dr, Orlando, FL 32819

Description: This budget-friendly accommodation near Universal Orlando Resort offers a welcoming environment for all travelers, including those from the LGBTQ+ community. The Econo Lodge offers basic amenities and a safe, friendly atmosphere.

Costs: Rates start at $50–$90 per night.

Contact: +1 (407) 351-3000

Website: Econo Lodge International Drive

Etiquette: As a budget option, guests are encouraged to respect other guests and maintain the quiet atmosphere in hallways and shared spaces.

Unique Stays and Experiences Near Universal Orlando Resort

For travelers seeking a distinctive and memorable stay, here are some unique guesthouses, B&Bs, and local lodgings that offer an alternative to traditional hotels near Universal Orlando Resort.

1. The Castle Hotel, Autograph Collection

Location: 8600 Universal Blvd, Orlando, FL 32819

Description: The Castle Hotel offers a unique experience with its European-inspired design, including turrets and elegant décor. It's perfect for guests looking for a fairytale-like experience while being close to Universal Orlando Resort. The boutique feel of the hotel combined with luxurious amenities creates a distinctive stay.

Costs: Rates start at approximately $150–$250 per night.

Contact: +1 (407) 996-7300

Website: The Castle Hotel

Etiquette: The Castle Hotel is a tranquil setting, so guests should maintain a calm and respectful attitude, especially in common areas like the courtyard and restaurant. Proper dress code is appreciated in dining areas.

2. The Enclave Hotel & Suites

Location: 6165 Carrier Dr, Orlando, FL 32819

Description: The Enclave offers a more intimate, comfortable stay with suites featuring kitchenettes, ideal for longer stays. It combines the warmth of a family-run atmosphere with the convenience of proximity to Universal Orlando Resort. Perfect for families or groups seeking space and privacy.

Costs: Rates begin at $80–$130 per night.

Contact: +1 (407) 351-5009

Website: The Enclave Hotel & Suites

Etiquette: Respect for other guests is crucial, especially in shared spaces like the pool or breakfast area. Guests should keep noise to a minimum and adhere to quiet hours in the evenings.

3. Park Plaza Hotel

Location: 300 S Park Ave, Winter Park, FL 32789 (About 20 minutes from Universal)

Description: Situated in the charming town of Winter Park, this boutique hotel offers a mix of vintage charm and modern amenities. Known for its personalized service, the Park Plaza Hotel offers a peaceful, relaxed stay while being a short drive from the bustling Universal Orlando Resort.

Costs: Rates typically range from $150–$250 per night.

Contact: +1 (407) 645-1828

Website: Park Plaza Hotel

Etiquette: With its historic setting, guests are encouraged to respect the classic architecture and enjoy the ambiance quietly. The hotel emphasizes relaxation and a calm atmosphere.

4. The Greenhouse Inn

Location: 214 E New Haven Ave, Melbourne, FL 32901 (A little over an hour drive from Universal Orlando)

Description: For a more personalized and nature-inspired stay, The Greenhouse Inn offers a cozy B&B experience. Located in Melbourne, it features eco-friendly practices, a peaceful garden, and homey accommodations. Ideal for travelers seeking a slower pace and an intimate setting.

Costs: Rates start at $150–$220 per night.

Contact: +1 (321) 723-5150

Website: The Greenhouse Inn

Etiquette: The Greenhouse Inn promotes sustainable tourism, so guests are encouraged to follow eco-friendly practices like minimizing energy use and recycling. Respect for the quiet atmosphere is essential.

5. Bamboo Garden Boutique Hotel

Location: 1770 West Hwy 192, Kissimmee, FL 34746 (15-minute drive from Universal Orlando)

Description: A unique retreat offering lush tropical gardens, a peaceful environment, and a blend of Asian-inspired décor. This boutique hotel is a hidden gem with intimate, personalized service, ideal for those looking to escape the typical tourist hustle.

Costs: Rates range from $120–$180 per night.

Contact: +1 (407) 507-5319

Website: Bamboo Garden Boutique Hotel

Etiquette: Guests should maintain a tranquil atmosphere by respecting the serene gardens and quiet spaces. The hotel encourages mindfulness and relaxation, so noise levels should be kept to a minimum, especially in outdoor areas.

6. Moss Park B&B

Location: 1300 N Alafaya Trail, Orlando, FL 32828 (A 25-minute drive from Universal)

Description: For travelers who enjoy nature and privacy, Moss Park offers a cozy bed-and-breakfast experience. Surrounded by lush greenery, the B&B offers a rural escape with an emphasis on local food and hospitality. Ideal for those who prefer a homey, quieter stay.

Costs: Rates start at $90–$150 per night.

Contact: +1 (407) 483-2200

Website: Moss Park B&B

Etiquette: As a quieter, nature-centered stay, guests should respect the natural surroundings and follow all house rules related to quiet times and outdoor areas.

7. Coco Key Water Resort

Location: 7400 International Dr, Orlando, FL 32819

Description: Although a more commercial property, Coco Key offers a fun, family-friendly experience with a water park included. For guests seeking a unique, adventurous experience with kids, this resort's tropical-themed water attractions provide an unforgettable stay.

Costs: Rates range from $100–$160 per night.

Contact: +1 (407) 351-3500

Website: Coco Key Water Resort

Etiquette: Guests are encouraged to enjoy the water park responsibly, with a focus on family-friendly behavior. Noise levels should be kept moderate, especially in the dining and pool areas.

8. The Thirsty Fish Hostel

Location: 30 E Central Blvd, Orlando, FL 32801

Description: For a more budget-conscious and social experience, The Thirsty Fish Hostel offers dorm-style accommodations with a community vibe. It's ideal for younger travelers or solo adventurers looking to meet new people. The hostel's proximity to downtown Orlando provides easy access to local attractions.

Costs: Rates begin at $30–$70 per night (for shared rooms).

Contact: +1 (407) 555-1234

Website: The Thirsty Fish Hostel

Etiquette: Hostel etiquette includes respecting other guests' quiet hours, keeping personal items organized, and maintaining a friendly and respectful attitude toward others in shared spaces.

9. Lake Buena Vista Resort Village & Spa

Location: 8102 Resort Village Dr, Orlando, FL 32821

Description: A stunning, Mediterranean-style resort village offering a unique stay with spacious condos and a full-service spa. With easy access to both Universal Orlando Resort and Walt Disney World, it's a great option for those looking for a more laid-back, residential-style lodging.

Costs: Rates typically range from $150–$250 per night.

Contact: +1 (407) 238-6500

Website: Lake Buena Vista Resort

Etiquette: Respect for fellow guests and maintaining quiet in common areas, especially around the pool and spa, is important for maintaining the peaceful ambiance.

Chapter 5: Experiencing Universal Orlando Resort

Must-See Attractions and Landmarks Near Universal Orlando Resort

Here is a curated list of key attractions and landmarks near Universal Orlando Resort, showcasing natural wonders, historical landmarks, and popular sites that make this region unique.

1. Universal Studios Florida

Location: 6000 Universal Blvd, Orlando, FL 32819

Description: One of the world's most famous theme parks, Universal Studios Florida is home to exciting attractions based on popular movies and TV shows. It's a must-visit for fans of everything from Harry Potter to The Simpsons.

Costs: Single-day tickets range from $109–$150, depending on the season.

Contact: +1 (407) 363-8000

Website: Universal Studios Florida

Etiquette: Guests are expected to follow park rules, such as staying in designated areas and respecting others in lines and attractions. Tipping at restaurants and for services is appreciated.

2. Universal's Islands of Adventure

Location: 6000 Universal Blvd, Orlando, FL 32819

Description: This theme park is perfect for thrill-seekers, featuring thrilling rides like The Incredible Hulk Coaster and the Jurassic Park River Adventure. It's also home to The Wizarding World of Harry Potter.

Costs: Tickets start at $109–$150 for a one-day pass.

Contact: +1 (407) 363-8000

Website: Islands of Adventure

Etiquette: Respect park guidelines, especially around rides, and be mindful of your surroundings to avoid crowding or blocking pathways.

3. Lake Eola Park

Location: 512 E Washington St, Orlando, FL 32801

Description: A beautiful park in downtown Orlando featuring a large lake, swan boats, and scenic walking paths. It's a relaxing place to enjoy nature and take in the beauty of the city.

Costs: Free to enter. Swan boat rentals cost approximately $15 for 30 minutes.

Contact: +1 (407) 246-4484

Website: Lake Eola Park

Etiquette: Visitors should maintain a peaceful atmosphere, avoid littering, and respect wildlife, especially the swans. Noise should be kept to a minimum.

4. ICON Park

Location: 8375 International Dr, Orlando, FL 32819

Description: ICON Park is home to The Wheel, a 400-foot-tall observation wheel offering stunning views of the Orlando skyline. The park also features shops, restaurants, and entertainment.

Costs: Tickets for The Wheel start at $30 per adult, with family packages available.

Contact: +1 (407) 601-7907

Website: ICON Park

Etiquette: Guests should adhere to safety guidelines when riding The Wheel and be respectful of others when exploring the park and dining areas.

5. The Wizarding World of Harry Potter

Location: 6000 Universal Blvd, Orlando, FL 32819 (Located within both Universal Studios Florida and Islands of Adventure)

Description: An immersive experience for Harry Potter fans, this attraction allows visitors to explore the magical world of Hogwarts, Diagon Alley, and more. Enjoy themed rides, shops, and restaurants like the Leaky Cauldron.

Costs: Requires a park-to-park ticket to access both Hogsmeade and Diagon Alley. Prices start at $164 for a one-day, two-park ticket.

Contact: +1 (407) 363-8000

Website: Wizarding World of Harry Potter

Etiquette: Be courteous in lines and on rides, and respect the magical atmosphere by refraining from loud or disruptive behavior. Photography is allowed, but flash photography is restricted on some rides.

6. Kennedy Space Center

Location: Space Commerce Way, Merritt Island, FL 32953 (Approx. 45-minute drive from Universal Orlando Resort)

Description: The Kennedy Space Center offers a fascinating journey through the history of space exploration. Visit the Space Shuttle Atlantis, meet astronauts, and learn about NASA's missions.

Costs: Tickets start at $57 for adults and $47 for children.

Contact: +1 (321) 449-4400

Website: Kennedy Space Center

Etiquette: Photography is encouraged but should be done in designated areas. Guests should respect exhibits and stay within designated areas during astronaut meet-and-greets.

7. Gatorland

Location: 14501 S Orange Blossom Trail, Orlando, FL 32837

Description: Known as the "Alligator Capital of the World," Gatorland is home to thousands of alligators, crocodiles, and other wildlife. The park also features live shows and opportunities for animal encounters.

Costs: Tickets start at $32.99 for adults and $22.99 for children.

Contact: +1 (800) 393-5297

Website: Gatorland

Etiquette: Guests should maintain a safe distance from the animals, respect the trainers during live shows, and avoid loud noises that could disturb the animals.

8. Orlando Science Center

Location: 777 E Princeton St, Orlando, FL 32803

Description: This family-friendly science museum offers interactive exhibits, live science shows, and planetarium shows. It's a great place to learn about science, space, and technology.

Costs: General admission starts at $21 for adults and $16 for children.

Contact: +1 (407) 514-2000

Website: Orlando Science Center

Etiquette: Please refrain from loud or disruptive behavior in exhibits, particularly in the planetarium. Be respectful of other guests, especially during interactive displays.

9. Old Town Kissimmee

Location: 5770 W Irlo Bronson Memorial Hwy, Kissimmee, FL 34746

Description: A charming, nostalgic spot offering classic car shows, rides, restaurants, and shopping. It's a place to enjoy traditional Americana in a vintage setting, with events like the Saturday night classic car parade.

Costs: Admission is free. Rides typically cost $3–$5 per person.

Contact: +1 (407) 396-4888

Website: Old Town Kissimmee

Etiquette: Keep noise levels low, especially during car shows and events. Respect the space of others while shopping or enjoying the outdoor attractions.

10. Harry P. Leu Gardens

Location: 1920 N Forest Ave, Orlando, FL 32803

Description: A beautiful 50-acre garden in the heart of Orlando, perfect for nature lovers. The garden features themed areas, walking paths, and a variety of plant species.

Costs: Admission is $10 for adults and $5 for children.

Contact: +1 (407) 246-2620

Website: Harry P. Leu Gardens

Etiquette: Guests should remain on paths, respect the plant life, and avoid loud noises to maintain the peaceful atmosphere.

Activities and Experiences Near Universal Orlando Resort

Here is a list of immersive activities and experiences that will enhance your visit to the Orlando area, offering everything from outdoor adventures to food tours and cultural workshops. Each option provides a unique way to experience the local culture, cuisine, and natural beauty.

1. Gatorland Zip Line

Location: 14501 S Orange Blossom Trail, Orlando, FL 32837

Description: Experience the thrill of zip-lining over thousands of alligators and crocodiles at Gatorland. This unique adventure provides aerial views of the park's wildlife, including its famous alligator breeding marsh.

Costs: $49.99 for a single zip line ride; combination passes with general admission available for $64.99.

Contact: +1 (800) 393-5297

Website: Gatorland Zip Line

Etiquette: Follow all safety guidelines and instructions from the staff. Respect the wildlife by maintaining a safe distance and avoiding loud noises that could disturb the animals.

2. Eco-Tours in the Everglades

Location: Everglades National Park (Approx. 1.5 hours drive from Orlando)

Description: Take a guided airboat tour through the Everglades to see the unique wildlife and lush vegetation of Florida's wetlands. These tours offer an up-close view of alligators, birds, and other local wildlife in their natural habitat.

Costs: Airboat tours start at $25 per person.

Contact: +1 (305) 247-2628

Website: Everglades National Park

Etiquette: Stay seated and remain calm during the tour. Do not feed or try to interact with the animals. Avoid littering and respect the natural environment.

3. Orlando Food Tours

Location: Various locations across Orlando (e.g., Winter Park, Downtown Orlando)

Description: Explore Orlando's culinary scene with a guided food tour. Sample local dishes, from Southern comfort food to fresh seafood, while learning about the city's food culture and history.

Costs: Tours start around $55–$85 per person.

Contact: +1 (407) 557-4525

Website: Orlando Food Tours

Etiquette: Be punctual, as tours typically run on a set schedule. Always ask before taking photos in restaurants or of dishes. Respect local dining etiquette, and feel free to ask questions about the dishes you're trying.

4. Dr. Phillips Center for the Performing Arts

Location: 445 S Magnolia Ave, Orlando, FL 32801

Description: Enjoy world-class performances, from Broadway shows to ballet, orchestras, and contemporary music at the Dr. Phillips Center. This venue hosts an array of cultural events throughout the year.

Costs: Ticket prices range from $25–$150 depending on the performance.

Contact: +1 (407) 839-0119

Website: Dr. Phillips Center

Etiquette: Arrive early to avoid missing the performance. During shows, refrain from talking or using your phone, and respect the performers and fellow attendees by maintaining silence during performances.

5. Cultural and Art Workshops at the Orlando Museum of Art

Location: 2416 N Mills Ave, Orlando, FL 32803

Description: Engage in hands-on art workshops at the Orlando Museum of Art, where you can create your own masterpieces while learning about local and international artists.

Costs: Workshops typically cost $25–$50 per session.

Contact: +1 (407) 896-4231

Website: Orlando Museum of Art

Etiquette: Keep noise to a minimum during workshops. Respect the space and materials, and be mindful of other participants. Clean up after your session and follow any additional instructions from the staff.

6. Wekiwa Springs State Park

Location: 1800 Wekiwa Cir, Apopka, FL 32712 (Approx. 30-minute drive from Orlando)

Description: A tranquil retreat offering outdoor activities like kayaking, hiking, and swimming in crystal-clear spring water. The park is known for its natural beauty, making it an ideal spot for relaxation and nature immersion.

Costs: Entry is $6 per vehicle.

Contact: +1 (407) 884-2008

Website: Wekiwa Springs State Park

Etiquette: Respect the park's wildlife and stay on marked trails. Pack out all trash and avoid using any watercraft in areas designated for swimming. Noise should be kept to a minimum to preserve the peaceful atmosphere.

7. Orlando Balloon Rides

Location: 4000 S. Orange Ave, Suite 204, Orlando, FL 32806

Description: Experience Orlando from above with a hot air balloon ride, offering breathtaking views of the city and surrounding areas at sunrise. This is a perfect activity for special occasions or a peaceful adventure.

Costs: Rides typically range from $190–$250 per person.

Contact: +1 (407) 363-6025

Website: Orlando Balloon Rides

Etiquette: Be on time for your scheduled flight, and follow all safety instructions from your pilot. Avoid any distractions that might hinder the pilot's ability to operate the balloon safely.

8. Lake Buena Vista Factory Stores

Location: 15657 S Apopka Vineland Rd, Orlando, FL 32821

Description: Shop for discounted designer goods at this outlet mall, featuring over 50 stores offering fashion, accessories, and home goods at lower prices. The mall also hosts events throughout the year.

Costs: Prices vary depending on the store and items you purchase.

Contact: +1 (407) 239-2100

Website: Lake Buena Vista Factory Stores

Etiquette: Respect store hours and return policies. Keep noise to a minimum in store areas and be mindful of personal space while shopping.

9. Orlando Tree Trek Adventure Park

Location: 7625 W Irlo Bronson Memorial Hwy, Kissimmee, FL 34747

Description: An exciting outdoor adventure park where visitors can challenge themselves on zip lines, rope courses, and other physical activities designed for all skill levels.

Costs: Admission starts at $34.99 for adults and $24.99 for children.

Contact: +1 (407) 390-9999

Website: Orlando Tree Trek

Etiquette: Respect the park's rules for safety and behavior. Maintain proper attire and footwear suitable for outdoor activities, and stay within your skill level to ensure a safe and enjoyable experience.

10. Sunshine Helicopter Tour

Location: 3450 S. Orange Ave, Orlando, FL 32806

Description: Experience Orlando from a new perspective with a helicopter tour. Fly over top attractions like Universal Orlando Resort, Walt Disney World, and the stunning landscape of Central Florida.

Costs: Prices for helicopter tours start at $40 for a 5-minute ride and up to $150 for a full tour.

Contact: +1 (407) 850-7380

Website: Sunshine Helicopter Tours

Etiquette: Arrive early for your flight and be on time. Follow safety instructions provided by the pilot, and keep noise levels low to avoid disturbing others during the flight.

Festivals and Events in Orlando

Orlando is known for its vibrant cultural scene, offering a variety of music, art, and cultural festivals throughout the year. Here are some of the top festivals and events you shouldn't miss during your visit to Universal Orlando Resort and the surrounding areas:

1. Epcot International Flower & Garden Festival

Location: Epcot, Walt Disney World Resort, 200 Epcot Center Dr, Lake Buena Vista, FL 32821

Description: Held annually from March to June, this festival celebrates the beauty of flowers and horticulture with breathtaking topiaries, gardens, and flower displays. The festival also includes outdoor kitchens with seasonal dishes and live music performances from popular bands.

Costs: Admission to the festival is included with Epcot park tickets (starting around $109 for one-day entry).

Contact: +1 (407) 939-5277

Website: Epcot International Flower & Garden Festival

Etiquette: Follow all park guidelines and respect the gardens by staying on designated paths. Be mindful of others while enjoying the displays and food offerings.

2. Mardi Gras at Universal Orlando Resort

Location: Universal Studios Florida, 6000 Universal Blvd, Orlando, FL 32819

Description: Celebrate the spirit of New Orleans at Universal Orlando's Mardi Gras celebration, typically held from February to April. The event features a grand parade, live music, and delicious Cajun cuisine. Guests can also enjoy performances from famous musicians and participate in themed parties throughout the park.

Costs: Admission to Mardi Gras events is included with regular park tickets.

Contact: +1 (407) 363-8000

Website: Mardi Gras at Universal Orlando

Etiquette: Be respectful during parades and performances, and participate in the festivities responsibly. Respect others' space during the celebrations, especially in crowded areas.

3. Florida Film Festival

Location: Enzian Theater, 1300 S Orlando Ave, Maitland, FL 32751 (About 20 minutes from Universal Orlando Resort)

Description: Held annually in April, the Florida Film Festival is one of the premier film festivals in the state, showcasing independent films, documentaries, and short films. This event celebrates cinema and brings filmmakers, industry professionals, and movie lovers together for screenings, discussions, and awards.

Costs: Tickets for individual screenings range from $12 to $20. Passes for multiple screenings are available.

Contact: +1 (407) 629-1088

Website: Florida Film Festival

Etiquette: Arrive early for screenings to secure the best seats. Silence your phones and avoid talking during films. Participate in Q&A sessions after the screenings if available.

4. Orlando International Fringe Theatre Festival

Location: Loch Haven Park, 777 E Princeton St, Orlando, FL 32803

Description: The Orlando Fringe Festival, held each May, is a renowned performing arts festival featuring hundreds of theater performances, musicals, improv shows, and art installations. It's an open-access event, meaning that anyone can participate, making it a great way to experience Orlando's diverse arts scene.

Costs: Admission to individual performances typically ranges from $12 to $20.

Contact: +1 (407) 648-0077

Website: Orlando International Fringe Theatre Festival

Etiquette: Be respectful to performers and fellow audience members. Arrive on time for shows, and silence your phone. Always check the festival program for specific performance rules.

5. Sunset Walk at Margaritaville Resort Orlando

Location: 8000 Fins Up Cir, Kissimmee, FL 34747

Description: Enjoy live music, entertainment, and a laid-back atmosphere at this annual festival, held every Saturday evening at Margaritaville Resort. You can explore local artisans, enjoy food trucks, and listen to a variety of live performances, from rock bands to solo acts.

Costs: Free entry; food and drinks are available for purchase.

Contact: +1 (407) 479-1182

Website: Margaritaville Resort Orlando Sunset Walk

Etiquette: While exploring the event, respect the vendors and artists. Be courteous to other attendees by avoiding loud conversations during performances.

6. Orlando Pride Festival

Location: Lake Eola Park, 512 E Washington St, Orlando, FL 32801

Description: Orlando's annual LGBTQ+ Pride Festival celebrates diversity and inclusion with a parade, live performances, food vendors, and community celebrations. Held each October, the event aims to bring awareness to LGBTQ+ rights and culture while offering a fun and engaging environment for all visitors.

Costs: Entry to the festival is free, but VIP passes and special events may have additional costs.

Contact: +1 (407) 539-8743

Website: Orlando Pride Festival

Etiquette: Be respectful and inclusive. Avoid disruptive behavior and embrace the positive, celebratory atmosphere. Follow all safety protocols, especially if attending in crowded areas.

7. Epcot International Food & Wine Festival

Location: Epcot, Walt Disney World Resort, 200 Epcot Center Dr, Lake Buena Vista, FL 32821

Description: One of the largest food festivals in the world, this event takes place in the fall, typically from late summer to early November. Guests can explore international cuisines, attend cooking demonstrations, and sample wines and cocktails from around the world.

Costs: Admission to the festival is included with Epcot park tickets. Food and drink tastings are available for purchase.

Contact: +1 (407) 939-5277

Website: Epcot International Food & Wine Festival

Etiquette: Respect the chefs and performers. Be mindful of portion sizes when tasting food to allow others the chance to try different dishes. Follow all park guidelines regarding food and beverage consumption.

8. Central Florida Jazz Festival

Location: Various venues in Downtown Orlando

Description: Celebrate jazz music with performances from top national and international artists at this annual event, usually held in March. The festival features multiple days of jazz concerts and community events.

Costs: Entry prices vary depending on the performance venue, with some events offering free entry.

Contact: +1 (407) 246-4484

Website: Central Florida Jazz Festival

Etiquette: Maintain respect for musicians and other attendees during performances. No talking or using cell phones during concerts.

Nightlife and Entertainment in Orlando

Orlando offers a diverse nightlife scene, catering to all types of travelers with vibrant nightclubs, cozy bars, exciting live music venues, and thrilling theater performances. Here's a look at some of the best nightlife and entertainment spots around Universal Orlando Resort:

1. Universal CityWalk

Location: 6000 Universal Blvd, Orlando, FL 32819

Description: CityWalk is Orlando's epicenter of nightlife, with a wide array of clubs, bars, and restaurants offering music and entertainment. You can enjoy live performances, dance the night away at the Hard Rock Live, or grab a drink at the many themed bars like the Red Coconut Club.

Costs: Free entry; drinks and food prices vary by venue.

Contact: +1 (407) 224-2691

Website: Universal CityWalk

Etiquette: Be respectful of other guests, especially in busy areas. Keep your noise levels considerate to ensure everyone enjoys the nightlife experience. Follow any dress codes and age restrictions.

2. The Edison

Location: 1490 E Buena Vista Dr, Lake Buena Vista, FL 32830 (Disney Springs)

Description: A unique blend of industrial glamour and 1920s steampunk, The Edison is a popular nightlife spot featuring live music, signature cocktails, and a great atmosphere. This venue often hosts themed events, cabaret performances, and even burlesque shows.

Costs: Entry is free, but drinks range from $10 to $15.

Contact: +1 (407) 560-9999

Website: The Edison

Etiquette: Dress smart-casual or in evening attire for a more upscale experience. Maintain respectful behavior during performances and while mingling in the space.

3. Raglan Road Irish Pub & Restaurant

Location: 1640 E Buena Vista Dr, Lake Buena Vista, FL 32830 (Disney Springs)

Description: Known for its lively Irish atmosphere, Raglan Road offers traditional pub fare, drinks, and live music every night. Enjoy the high-energy performances by Irish dancers and musicians, making it a perfect place for a fun night out.

Costs: Entry is free; drinks start at around $8. Food prices vary, with entrees from $15 to $30.

Contact: +1 (407) 938-0300

Website: Raglan Road Irish Pub

Etiquette: Respect the performers and staff. Avoid disruptive behavior during performances, and be mindful of the space around the live music areas.

4. Dr. Phillips Center for the Performing Arts

Location: 445 S Magnolia Ave, Orlando, FL 32801

Description: For a more refined night out, head to the Dr. Phillips Center, where you can enjoy Broadway shows, symphonies, ballets, and concerts by world-renowned performers. It's the premier venue for arts lovers in Orlando.

Costs: Ticket prices for shows vary, with performances ranging from $30 to $150 depending on the event.

Contact: +1 (407) 839-0119

Website: Dr. Phillips Center

Etiquette: Arrive on time for performances. No talking during shows, and silence your phone to avoid disturbing others. Dress appropriately for the event.

5. House of Blues Orlando

Location: 1490 E Buena Vista Dr, Lake Buena Vista, FL 32830 (Disney Springs)

Description: House of Blues is a live music venue offering concerts from a wide range of genres, from rock to blues and country. The venue also features a bar and restaurant, making it a great place for a night of food, drinks, and music.

Costs: Entry varies by event, with most tickets ranging from $15 to $50.

Contact: +1 (407) 934-2583

Website: House of Blues Orlando

Etiquette: Respect the crowd and performers during shows. Avoid blocking views and be mindful of noise levels when the music is playing. Maintain good behavior in the restaurant and bar areas.

6. The Social

Location: 54 N Orange Ave, Orlando, FL 32801

Description: One of Orlando's top live music venues, The Social features indie bands, rock performances, and electronic music in an intimate setting. It's a favorite among locals for its laid-back yet energetic vibe.

Costs: Entry generally costs around $10 to $25, depending on the performer.

Contact: +1 (407) 246-1419

Website: The Social

Etiquette: Be courteous to other concert-goers and avoid pushing or shoving in the crowd. Be aware of your surroundings and respect the venue's policies.

7. Cuba Libre Restaurant & Rum Bar

Location: 9101 International Dr, Orlando, FL 32819

Description: Known for its Latin-inspired cocktails and lively atmosphere, Cuba Libre offers a mix of Cuban food, music, and dancing. Guests can enjoy salsa dancing on weekends, making it a great spot for those looking to enjoy Latin nightlife.

Costs: Drinks start at $8, and entrees are priced between $15 and $30.

Contact: +1 (407) 226-1600

Website: Cuba Libre

Etiquette: Embrace the lively vibe, but be respectful on the dance floor. Be mindful of others' space, especially when dancing, and follow any dress codes for the venue.

8. SAK Comedy Lab

Location: 29 S Orange Ave, Orlando, FL 32801

Description: SAK Comedy Lab offers improv comedy shows that promise to make you laugh all night. It's a great choice for those looking for a fun and relaxed evening with some humor and lighthearted entertainment.

Costs: Tickets are around $15 to $30 per person.

Contact: +1 (407) 648-0001

Website: SAK Comedy Lab

Etiquette: Enjoy the show by keeping distractions to a minimum. Avoid talking loudly during performances, and participate in the fun by being responsive to the improvisational comedy.

Shopping and Souvenirs in Orlando

Orlando is not only a destination for thrill-seekers but also for those who love to shop. From high-end malls to local markets, there's a wide variety of shopping experiences to enjoy. Here's a guide to the best shopping areas, markets, and tips for finding local crafts in the city:

1. Disney Springs

Location: 1486 E Buena Vista Dr, Lake Buena Vista, FL 32830

Description: Disney Springs is a shopping and entertainment complex that offers an array of stores, including Disney-themed shops, high-end brands, and unique boutiques. It's a great place to find exclusive Disney merchandise, clothing, jewelry, and artwork.

Costs: Prices vary widely, with Disney-themed items starting at $10, and luxury items priced from $50 to several hundred dollars.

Contact: +1 (407) 828-4000

Website: Disney Springs

Etiquette: Be respectful of the crowded areas, especially during peak times. Consider the dress code in certain stores, and refrain from loud talking while shopping.

2. The Mall at Millenia

Location: 4200 Conroy Rd, Orlando, FL 32839

Description: One of Orlando's premier shopping destinations, this upscale mall features luxury stores like Gucci, Chanel, and Louis Vuitton, alongside more affordable options like Zara and H&M. It's the perfect place for high-end shopping and to pick up souvenirs.

Costs: Expect to pay anywhere from $20 for casual wear to several hundred dollars for luxury goods.

Contact: +1 (407) 363-3555

Website: The Mall at Millenia

Etiquette: Maintain a polite demeanor when browsing luxury goods and dress smart-casual. Follow store policies, particularly in high-end stores where handling of items may be restricted.

3. Orlando International Premium Outlets

Location: 4951 International Dr, Orlando, FL 32819

Description: A popular outlet mall featuring a wide selection of designer brands at discounted prices. It's a great place for budget-conscious shoppers to find high-quality clothing, shoes, and accessories from brands like Nike, Michael Kors, and Coach.

Costs: Discounts range from 25% to 70% off retail prices. Expect to pay around $20-$100 for most items.

Contact: +1 (407) 351-2750

Website: Orlando International Premium Outlets

Etiquette: Respect the store staff and be courteous while looking through discounted goods. Handle merchandise with care, especially in busy sales areas.

4. International Drive (I-Drive)

Location: International Drive, Orlando, FL

Description: A bustling area with various shopping options, from souvenir shops to boutiques and department stores. It's the ideal location for finding Disney and Universal Studios memorabilia, as well as unique items from local artisans.

Costs: Souvenirs and trinkets typically range from $5 to $50, depending on the item. Higher-end boutique items may cost more.

Contact: Varies by store

Website: International Drive

Etiquette: Be respectful in smaller shops and markets. Bargaining is not common, but it's always polite to thank the vendor for their time.

5. Winter Park Farmers' Market

Location: 200 W New England Ave, Winter Park, FL 32789

Description: A great spot for locally crafted goods, the Winter Park Farmers' Market features fresh produce, handmade crafts, jewelry, and artwork. It's an excellent place to pick up unique, locally-made souvenirs.

Costs: Prices for crafts and goods range from $10 for small items to $100 for larger handcrafted works.

Contact: +1 (407) 599-3342

Website: Winter Park Farmers' Market

Etiquette: Respect local vendors and the marketplace environment. Always ask about the origin of crafts if you're curious, as many items are handcrafted by local artisans.

6. Kissimmee Old Town

Location: 5770 W Irlo Bronson Memorial Hwy, Kissimmee, FL 34746

Description: This charming shopping area features vintage shops, craft stores, and local vendors selling unique souvenirs, including nostalgic toys, classic Florida-themed items, and handmade jewelry.

Costs: Expect to find items for as low as $5 for small trinkets to $50 or more for special, one-of-a-kind pieces.

Contact: +1 (407) 396-4888

Website: Kissimmee Old Town

Etiquette: Enjoy browsing at your own pace and engage with local vendors in a friendly manner. It's a more relaxed environment, but still polite and courteous.

7. East End Market

Location: 3201 Corrine Dr, Orlando, FL 32803

Description: A local market that celebrates Orlando's artisans, farmers, and makers, East End Market offers a great selection of handcrafted goods, locally sourced food, and unique gifts. It's perfect for finding distinctive souvenirs and supporting local businesses.

Costs: Handmade goods range from $10 for small trinkets to $100 for larger artisanal pieces.

Contact: +1 (407) 281-0713

Website: East End Market

Etiquette: Engage with local artisans and vendors respectfully. Appreciate the craft behind the handmade items and ask questions about the products you're interested in.

Chapter 6: Practical Information for Travelers

Currency, Money Matters, and Travel Insurance in Orlando

When visiting Orlando, understanding how to manage your currency, exchange rates, and securing travel insurance will make your trip smoother and more financially manageable. Here's a guide to help with these important financial aspects:

1. Currency in Orlando

Currency Used: The United States Dollar (USD) is the official currency in Orlando.

Coins: Pennies (1¢), Nickels (5¢), Dimes (10¢), Quarters (25¢), Half Dollars (50¢), and Dollar Coins ($1).

Paper Money: $1, $5, $10, $20, $50, and $100 bills.

Exchange Rate: Exchange rates vary, so it's recommended to check the rate before converting money. Currency exchange services are available at airports, banks, and exchange counters around the city.

Where to Exchange Currency:

Orlando International Airport (MCO): Offers currency exchange services at various terminals. Expect slightly higher fees at the airport compared to other locations.

Banks: Major banks like Bank of America, Wells Fargo, and Chase have branches throughout the city where you can exchange money at competitive rates.

Currency Exchange Counters: Popular exchange services like Travelex can be found in malls and near tourist spots.

Contact:

Orlando International Airport: +1 (407) 825-2001

Travelex: Travelex

Bank of America: +1 (800) 432-1000

2. Handling Money in Orlando

ATMs: ATMs are widely available throughout Orlando, including at airports, malls, and hotels. Be mindful of foreign transaction fees your home bank might charge.

Credit and Debit Cards: Major credit cards like Visa, Mastercard, American Express, and Discover are widely accepted in most places. Debit cards can also be used for withdrawals at ATMs or payments, but be sure to notify your bank of your travel to avoid security holds.

Tipping: Tipping is customary in the U.S. and is typically 15-20% of the bill in restaurants. For taxis, tip around $1-$2 or 10-15%. Housekeeping and hotel staff should also be tipped, around $1-$5 per night.

Money Management Tips:

Carry Cash: While cards are accepted everywhere, it's helpful to have cash on hand for smaller purchases or in case a merchant doesn't accept cards.

Avoid Currency Exchange Scams: Be cautious of exchange services offering overly favorable rates. Stick to reputable sources like banks or official exchange counters.

3. Exchange Rate Tools

XE Currency App: Provides live exchange rate updates and helps with currency conversions. Available for free on both iOS and Android.

XE Currency App

OANDA: Offers reliable exchange rate information and is another helpful tool for checking real-time conversions.

OANDA

4. Travel Insurance

Why It's Important: Travel insurance protects you from unforeseen circumstances such as trip cancellations, medical emergencies, lost luggage, and travel delays. It's recommended to purchase travel insurance before departure to ensure full coverage.

Types of Coverage:

Trip Cancellation/Interruption: Covers the cost of your trip if you need to cancel or cut it short due to illness, weather conditions, or other covered reasons.

Medical and Emergency Services: Covers emergency medical expenses, hospital stays, and evacuation in case of illness or injury.

Lost or Stolen Property: Protects against lost luggage, personal belongings, or theft during travel.

Flight Delays and Missed Connections: Covers additional expenses if your flight is delayed or canceled.

Top Travel Insurance Providers:

Allianz Travel Insurance

Contact: +1 (800) 284-8300

Website: Allianz Travel Insurance

Travel Guard

Contact: +1 (800) 826-1300

Website: Travel Guard

World Nomads

Contact: +1 (877) 232-4983

Website: World Nomads

Insurance Tips:

Check Existing Coverage: Some credit cards offer limited travel insurance, so review the terms to see if you're already covered for some aspects of your trip.

Understand the Fine Print: Read the policy carefully to know what's covered, especially exclusions like pre-existing medical conditions, adventure sports, or natural disasters.

File Claims Promptly: If something goes wrong, contact your insurance provider immediately and file any necessary claims promptly to ensure timely resolution.

Dining and Cuisine in Orlando

Orlando offers a variety of dining experiences, from fast food to fine dining, with a wide selection of international and local cuisine. Here's a guide to the traditional dishes, must-try foods, and dining etiquette in Orlando:

1. Traditional Dishes and Must-Try Foods

Key Lime Pie: A dessert made with key lime juice, egg yolks, sweetened condensed milk, and a graham cracker crust. It's the perfect sweet and tangy treat to finish your meal.

Cuban Sandwich: A Florida favorite, especially in Orlando's Cuban community. This sandwich includes roast pork, ham, Swiss cheese, pickles, and mustard on Cuban bread.

Florida Grouper: Grouper is a popular fish in Florida, often served grilled or blackened. Try it as part of a fish taco or as an entrée.

Barbecue Ribs: Orlando has several Southern-style barbecue joints where tender, slow-cooked ribs are a must-try.

Fried Catfish: Common in Southern cuisine, fried catfish is served with sides like hushpuppies and coleslaw.

Gator Bites: If you're feeling adventurous, try fried alligator meat, often served with a spicy dipping sauce.

Cuban Coffee: Strong, sweet coffee that's served in small cups. It's a cultural staple, especially in Cuban restaurants and cafés in Orlando.

2. Top Restaurants and Dining Locations

The Ravenous Pig

Cuisine: American Gastropub, known for upscale comfort food.

Must-Try: Charcuterie board, fried chicken, and their craft cocktails.

Cost: $20 - $50 per person.

Location: 565 W Fairbanks Ave, Winter Park, FL.

Contact: +1 (407) 628-2333

Website: The Ravenous Pig

Victoria & Albert's

Cuisine: Fine Dining, located in Disney's Grand Floridian Resort & Spa.

Must-Try: Chef's Tasting Menu, which offers multiple courses with wine pairings.

Cost: $185 - $250 per person (depending on the menu).

Location: 4401 Grand Floridian Way, Lake Buena Vista, FL.

Contact: +1 (407) 824-2398

Website: Victoria & Albert's

Four Rivers Smokehouse

Cuisine: Southern Barbecue, specializing in smoked meats.

Must-Try: The brisket and the Texas-style sausage.

Cost: $10 - $20 per person.

Location: 1321 W Fairbanks Ave, Winter Park, FL.

Contact: +1 (407) 678-0940

Website: Four Rivers Smokehouse

Café Tu Tu Tango

Cuisine: Tapas, with a focus on small, shareable plates.

Must-Try: Signature sangria and artichoke dip.

Cost: $15 - $35 per person.

Location: 8625 International Dr, Orlando, FL.

Contact: +1 (407) 248-2222

Website: Café Tu Tu Tango

The Boathouse

Cuisine: Seafood, offering both casual and upscale options.

Must-Try: Lobster roll and crab cakes.

Cost: $30 - $60 per person.

Location: 1620 E Buena Vista Dr, Lake Buena Vista, FL.

Contact: +1 (407) 939-2628

Website: The Boathouse

3. Cost of Dining

Budget Meals: Fast food chains and local diners cost around $5-$15 per meal. Food trucks are also popular for quick, inexpensive bites.

Mid-Range Meals: Mid-tier restaurants will range between $15-$40 per person.

Fine Dining: Upscale restaurants or hotel dining can range from $50-$200 per person depending on the meal and location.

4. Dining Etiquette in Orlando

Tipping: Tipping is customary in the U.S. and should be around 15-20% of your total bill. In more casual settings, tips of $1-$2 per drink or item are also appreciated.

Reservations: It's advised to make reservations, especially for high-demand restaurants like Victoria & Albert's and The Boathouse, as Orlando can get quite busy with tourists year-round.

Casual Dining: For casual eateries, shorts and comfortable attire are fine. However, upscale restaurants like Victoria & Albert's require more formal attire (e.g., no shorts or tank tops).

Self-Service: Some casual spots may offer counter service, but for sit-down meals, expect to be seated and served by waitstaff.

Meal Times: Dinner service typically starts around 5 PM and goes until 10 PM, with peak dining times from 7 PM to 9 PM.

Special Dietary Needs: Most Orlando restaurants accommodate dietary restrictions such as gluten-free, vegetarian, vegan, or allergy-friendly meals. Don't hesitate to ask the server for options or substitutions.

safety tips for Solo, Group, and LGBTQ+ Travelers in Orlando, with advice tailored to each group

Here are safety tips for Solo, Group, and LGBTQ+ Travelers in Orlando, with advice tailored to each group:

1. Solo Travelers

Orlando is a popular destination for solo travelers, offering a wide range of activities and attractions. To ensure your safety while exploring, follow these tips:

General Tips:

Stay in Well-Lit Areas: Stick to areas that are well-lit, especially after dark. Popular areas like International Drive and Disney Springs are safe and active, with plenty of people around.

Share Your Itinerary: Let a friend or family member know your travel plans, including hotel details and daily itineraries. It's always wise to share your location via apps like Google Maps or Life360.

Use Trusted Transportation: Use rideshare services like Uber or Lyft instead of taxis, especially at night. Verify the car and driver details before entering.

Keep Valuables Safe: Carry minimal cash and keep your valuables secure, preferably in a hidden money belt or a locked hotel safe.

Trust Your Instincts: If something feels off, walk away. Trust your gut and seek assistance if needed.

Emergency Contact:

Orlando Police Department: +1 (407) 246-2470

Emergency Services (Police, Fire, Medical): 911

2. Group Travelers

Whether with friends or family, traveling in a group can be exciting, but it's important to prioritize safety, especially in crowded areas. Here's how to stay safe as a group:

General Tips:

Stay Together: While exploring, make sure no one gets left behind. Arrange meeting points if anyone gets separated. Stick together at night in places like Universal CityWalk or International Drive.

Know Your Limits: Whether it's alcohol consumption or physical activities, be mindful of everyone's limits. Don't push group members to do things they are not comfortable with.

Use Group Communication Apps: Apps like WhatsApp or GroupMe are great for staying connected, especially in busy tourist spots or theme parks. You can share live locations to ensure everyone stays on track.

Safety in Numbers: Traveling with a group means increased security. Avoid going into less populated or unfamiliar neighborhoods without the full group.

Emergency Contact for Groups:

Orlando Tourism Assistance: +1 (407) 363-5872

Florida Highway Patrol: +1 (407) 737-2213

3. LGBTQ+ Travelers

Orlando is known for being a welcoming and LGBTQ+-friendly destination, but it's always important to be aware of your surroundings and follow some safety tips for an enjoyable and stress-free experience.

General Tips:

Embrace Safe Spaces: Orlando offers LGBTQ+ safe spaces, including bars, clubs, and events like The Parliament House and Stonewall Bar. Familiarize yourself with these spaces and the local community.

Public Displays of Affection: While Orlando is LGBTQ+-friendly, always be mindful of your surroundings. Public displays of affection may be viewed differently in more conservative or quiet areas.

Respect Local Customs: Stick to popular, tourist-heavy areas like Lake Eola, Disney Springs, and Universal CityWalk for the best experience. These areas are more likely to be inclusive and welcoming.

Use LGBTQ+ Travel Resources: Apps and websites like GayTravel.com, Pinkster, and Visit Orlando's LGBTQ+ pages offer valuable information on LGBTQ+-friendly hotels, restaurants, and events.

Know Your Rights: Florida is relatively accepting, but it's always wise to be aware of your rights as an LGBTQ+ traveler, especially in areas where acceptance may vary.

LGBTQ+ Resources:

Orlando LGBTQ+ Chamber of Commerce: Orlando LGBTQ Chamber

Visit Orlando's LGBTQ+ Guide: Visit Orlando LGBTQ

General Safety Tips for All Travelers:

Emergency Numbers: Save the local emergency contact numbers in your phone.

Orlando Police Department: +1 (407) 246-2470

Fire Department: 911

Travel Insurance: Always ensure you have comprehensive travel insurance that covers theft, medical emergencies, and trip interruptions.

Stay Connected: Share your plans with someone and regularly check in with them.

Secure Personal Items: Avoid leaving your belongings unattended, and be cautious when using public Wi-Fi for sensitive activities like banking or shopping.

By following these safety tips, you can ensure that your trip to Orlando is as enjoyable and worry-free as possible, regardless of whether you're traveling solo, in a group, or as part of the LGBTQ+ community.

Wellness and Relaxation Options

Orlando offers a variety of wellness and relaxation options to help travelers unwind and recharge. Whether you're looking for a luxurious spa experience, a rejuvenating yoga session, or just a peaceful environment to relax, there are plenty of places to explore.

1. Spas and Wellness Centers

Orlando is home to several world-class spas that cater to both relaxation and rejuvenation. Many of these spas offer treatments designed to help you de-stress after a day of sightseeing or adventure.

Key Spas in Orlando:

The Ritz-Carlton Spa, Orlando
Location: 4012 Central Florida Parkway, Orlando, FL 32837
Cost: Treatments start from $150
Contact: +1 (407) 393-4200
Etiquette: Book in advance; gratuities are usually added to the bill.
Highlights: Offers luxurious spa treatments like facials, massages, and body wraps. Enjoy the serene atmosphere and expert care.

Mandara Spa at Walt Disney World Dolphin

Location: 1500 Epcot Resort Blvd, Lake Buena Vista, FL 32830
Cost: Treatments from $115
Contact: +1 (407) 934-4772
Etiquette: Reservations are recommended, especially during peak times.
Highlights: Known for its wide range of therapies, including aromatherapy massages and skin treatments. It's ideal for relaxation after a long day at the parks.

The Spa at Four Seasons Resort Orlando
Location: 10100 Dream Tree Blvd, Orlando, FL 32836
Cost: Services range from $150 to $300
Contact: +1 (407) 313-7777
Etiquette: Booking is required for treatments. Ensure to arrive 30 minutes early for relaxation.
Highlights: A tranquil oasis offering luxury services such as hot stone massages, facials, and even children's treatments.

2. Yoga and Meditation Centers

Orlando also offers several yoga studios and meditation centers where visitors can unwind, de-stress, and improve their mental well-being.

Notable Yoga and Meditation Centers:

Orlando Power Yoga
Location: 2586 E. Colonial Drive, Orlando, FL 32803
Cost: $20 per class or $120 for a 10-class pass
Contact: +1 (407) 228-2171
Etiquette: Arrive early to ensure a spot; wear comfortable clothing and bring your own mat.
Highlights: This studio offers a variety of yoga classes, including hot yoga, vinyasa, and restorative yoga for all skill levels.

Full Circle Yoga
Location: 4651 S. Kirkman Road, Orlando, FL 32811
Cost: $18 per class or $125 for a monthly pass
Contact: +1 (407) 982-9696
Etiquette: Silence your phone before class and be mindful of other participants.
Highlights: Known for its calm atmosphere and range of yoga styles, including hatha and power yoga. It's a great spot to connect with both your body and mind.

The Yoga Shala
Location: 1110 S. Orlando Ave., Winter Park, FL 32789
Cost: $16 per class
Contact: +1 (407) 601-1350
Etiquette: Please arrive at least 10 minutes before the class starts.

Highlights: A peaceful center offering classes in a range of yoga practices, including meditation and restorative yoga. The studio is intimate and perfect for a calming experience.

3. Hot Springs and Natural Relaxation Spots

While Orlando doesn't have traditional hot springs, there are nearby areas known for natural relaxation experiences, including scenic spots perfect for a peaceful retreat.

Nearby Hot Springs and Nature Retreats:

Wekiwa Springs State Park
Location: 1800 Wekiwa Circle, Apopka, FL 32712
Cost: Entrance fee is $6 per vehicle
Contact: +1 (407) 884-2008
Etiquette: Pack out all trash and respect the natural surroundings.
Highlights: While it doesn't feature hot springs, Wekiwa Springs offers crystal-clear waters perfect for swimming, kayaking, and hiking. It's a tranquil environment for a natural retreat.

Silver Springs State Park
Location: 1425 NE 58th Ave, Ocala, FL 34470
Cost: $2 per person for entry
Contact: +1 (352) 236-7143
Highlights: Known for its glass-bottom boat tours, this park is an excellent place to unwind with beautiful scenery and a peaceful atmosphere. While there are no hot springs, the area is a great way to connect with nature.

4. Relaxation and Wellness Resorts

For those seeking a comprehensive wellness retreat, Orlando is home to some luxury resorts where guests can enjoy both spa treatments and wellness-focused activities.

Lake Buena Vista Resort Village & Spa
Location: 8113 Resort Village Drive, Orlando, FL 32821
Cost: Rates start at $150 per night
Contact: +1 (407) 239-0000
Highlights: Offers a spa with an array of relaxation therapies, along with access to pools and wellness programs.

Grande Lakes Orlando (The Ritz-Carlton and JW Marriott)
Location: 4040 Central Florida Parkway, Orlando, FL 32837
Cost: Rates from $249 per night
Contact: +1 (407) 206-2400
Highlights: Home to both the Ritz-Carlton Spa and the JW Marriott's Spa, it offers everything from detox treatments to yoga classes, making it an excellent wellness destination.

5. Relaxation Tips and Etiquette

Book in Advance: Especially for spas and wellness centers, booking treatments ahead of time ensures availability.

Tip Generously: For most wellness services, a 15%-20% tip is standard. This can be given at the time of service or added to the bill.

Respect Quiet Zones: Many spas and wellness centers request guests to keep noise to a minimum to maintain a tranquil atmosphere.

Dress Comfortably: For yoga or meditation, wear loose, breathable clothing. For spas, most provide robes, but bring your own if you prefer.

Useful Contacts and Emergency Information

Here is a list of useful contacts and emergency information for travelers to Universal Orlando Resort:

Emergency Contacts:

Emergency Services (Police, Fire, Medical):
Dial: 911
Available: 24/7
Important: In case of an emergency, dial 911 for immediate help. Operators will provide assistance in English and Spanish.

Universal Orlando Resort Security
Contact: +1 (407) 363-8000
Available: 24/7
Important: For security-related inquiries or assistance within the resort, call Universal Security.

Orlando Poison Control Center
Contact: +1 (800) 222-1222
Available: 24/7
Important: Call immediately for any poisoning incidents or emergencies involving chemicals or toxins.

Fire and Rescue (Non-Emergency)
Contact: +1 (407) 246-2000
Available: 24/7
Important: For non-urgent fire or rescue inquiries.

Orlando Police Department
Contact: +1 (407) 246-2470
Available: 24/7

Important: For general law enforcement assistance or non-emergency inquiries.

Embassy Contacts (For International Travelers):

U.S. Embassy in the United Kingdom
Contact: +44 (0) 20 7499 9000
Website: https://uk.usembassy.gov
Hours: Monday to Friday, 8:30 AM – 5:30 PM
Important: For UK nationals or visitors requiring consular services.

U.S. Embassy in Canada
Contact: +1 (613) 688-5335
Website: https://ca.usembassy.gov
Hours: Monday to Friday, 8:30 AM – 5:00 PM
Important: For Canadian nationals or visitors requiring consular services.

U.S. Embassy in Mexico
Contact: +52 (55) 5280-3000
Website: https://mx.usembassy.gov
Hours: Monday to Friday, 8:00 AM – 4:30 PM
Important: For Mexican nationals or visitors requiring consular services.

U.S. Embassy in Australia
Contact: +61 (0) 2 9373 9200
Website: https://au.usembassy.gov
Hours: Monday to Friday, 8:30 AM – 5:00 PM
Important: For Australian nationals or visitors requiring consular services.

U.S. Embassy in Germany
Contact: +49 (0) 30 8305-0
Website: https://de.usembassy.gov
Hours: Monday to Friday, 8:30 AM – 5:30 PM
Important: For German nationals or visitors requiring consular services.

Health and Medical Resources:

Orlando Health – Medical Services
Contact: +1 (407) 303-2600
Available: 24/7
Website: https://www.orlandohealth.com
Important: Provides comprehensive medical services, including emergency care and specialized treatments.

Florida Hospital (AdventHealth)

Contact: +1 (407) 303-2200
Available: 24/7
Website: https://www.adventhealth.com
Important: Offers emergency care, urgent care, and outpatient services.

Urgent Care – FastMed Urgent Care
Location: 5033 Dr. Phillips Blvd, Suite 105, Orlando, FL 32819
Contact: +1 (407) 217-2170
Hours: Monday to Friday, 8:00 AM – 8:00 PM; Saturday-Sunday, 8:00 AM – 5:00 PM
Important: A convenient option for non-emergency medical needs.

Travel Assistance and Insurance Contacts:

Travel Insurance Services (InsureMyTrip)
Contact: +1 (800) 487-4722
Website: https://www.insuremytrip.com
Important: Provides travel insurance options, including coverage for medical emergencies, trip cancellations, and lost baggage.

Allianz Global Assistance
Contact: +1 (800) 654-1908
Website: https://www.allianztravelinsurance.com
Important: Offers comprehensive travel insurance plans with coverage for medical emergencies, trip interruptions, and other incidents.

Local Contacts and Other Resources:

Orlando International Airport (MCO)
Contact: +1 (407) 825-2001
Website: https://orlandoairports.net
Important: Provides flight, baggage, and airport assistance.

Universal Orlando Resort Guest Services
Contact: +1 (407) 224-4233
Website: https://www.universalorlando.com
Important: For general inquiries, accessibility services, and assistance while visiting Universal Orlando Resort.

Florida Highway Patrol (FHP)
Contact: +1 (407) 737-2213
Website: https://www.flhsmv.gov/fhp
Important: For highway safety and emergency road assistance in the state of Florida.

Important Travel Tips:

Always carry a photocopy of your passport and important documents, especially if traveling internationally.

Make sure to have travel insurance covering both medical emergencies and unexpected trip cancellations.

Keep emergency numbers saved in your phone and on paper for easy access in case of an emergency.

Always stay aware of your surroundings and follow local safety advice.

Money matters: currency exchange and budgeting tips.

Here's a guide on money matters for travelers visiting Universal Orlando Resort, including currency exchange, budgeting tips, and local etiquette:

Currency Exchange:

Currency:
The official currency in the United States is the U.S. Dollar (USD).
Exchange Rate: Rates fluctuate daily; check the current rate before exchanging currency.
Tip: It's best to exchange currency before arriving, but most international banks and exchange services offer competitive rates.

Currency Exchange Locations in Orlando:

1. Travelex at Orlando International Airport (MCO)
Location: Main terminal, Level 3, Orlando International Airport
Contact: +1 (407) 859-2305
Hours: 7:00 AM – 9:00 PM
Services: Currency exchange and international wire transfer services.
Fees: Exchange rates plus service fees.

2. Currency Exchange International (CEI)
Location: 4669 W Irlo Bronson Memorial Hwy, Kissimmee, FL 34746
Contact: +1 (407) 397-9990
Hours: Monday to Saturday, 9:00 AM – 6:00 PM
Services: Exchange, wire transfers, and prepaid travel cards.
Fees: Fees vary by transaction and amount.

3. Bank of America
Location: 151 N Orange Ave, Orlando, FL 32801
Contact: +1 (407) 839-1777
Services: Currency exchange services, ATM withdrawals for international cards.
Fees: Currency exchange fees apply.

Budgeting Tips:

1. Plan for Extra Costs: Always budget 10-20% more than anticipated for unexpected expenses like tips, souvenirs, and transportation.

2. ATMs for Cash Withdrawals: Use ATMs affiliated with major banks for better exchange rates, as opposed to airport ATMs, which often have higher fees.

3. Use Credit Cards with No Foreign Transaction Fees: These can save you money on exchanges and offer additional rewards.

4. Prepaid Travel Cards: Prepaid cards like Visa TravelMoney or American Express Prepaid Cards are convenient for budget control and can be used just like debit cards.

Important Currency Notes:

Small bills (1s, 5s, 10s) are useful for tipping and small transactions.

Tipping: Tipping is expected in the U.S. in most service situations. 15-20% is customary for restaurant bills. For bellhops or hotel service, $1-$2 per bag is appropriate.

Sales Tax: Florida's sales tax rate is 6.5%, but some areas (like Orange County) charge an additional 1.5%. Always check for tax-inclusive prices.

Budgeting for Universal Orlando Resort:

Universal Orlando Resort offers several packages, and budgeting is key for a good experience.

Cost Breakdown:

Ticket Prices:

One-Day Single Park Ticket: $109 - $159 (varies by date).

Park-to-Park Ticket (allows access to both Universal Studios and Islands of Adventure): $164 - $234.

VIP Experience: $179 - $279 per person (includes skip-the-line privileges).

Food and Dining:

Casual meals inside the parks average $15 - $25 per person.

Fine dining (e.g., at The Palm or Emeril's at CityWalk) can range from $50 - $100 per person.

Snack Costs: $3 - $8 per snack (e.g., ice cream, popcorn).

Souvenirs:

T-shirts: $20 - $40

Collectible items: $10 - $50

Unique experiences like character meet-and-greets or photo ops may cost $25 - $50.

Cash vs. Card:

Universal Orlando Resort accepts both credit cards and debit cards. Cash can also be used, but many areas (like shops and food carts) prefer cards.

ATMs are located throughout the resort, but fees may apply for non-network withdrawals.

Local Etiquette:

Tipping: As mentioned, tipping is important in the U.S.

Restaurants: 15-20% of the bill is standard.

Hotel Staff: $1-$2 per bag for bellhops, $1-$5 per night for housekeeping.

Valets: $2-$5 for valet parking services.

Bills and Sales Tax: Sales tax is added after the price. Be sure to check if it's included in the listed price (sometimes it's not).

Bargaining: In most places in the U.S., bargaining is not common practice, particularly in stores and restaurants. The prices are usually fixed.

Useful Contacts:

Travelex: +1 (407) 859-2305

Currency Exchange International (CEI): +1 (407) 397-9990

Bank of America (Currency Exchange): +1 (407) 839-1777

Universal Orlando Resort Customer Service: +1 (407) 224-4233

Important Links:

Universal Orlando Resort Website: www.universalorlando.com

Orlando Official Travel Guide (for general info): www.visitorlando.com

Final tips for a successful trip

Here are final tips to ensure you have a successful and enjoyable trip to Universal Orlando Resort:

1. Plan and Book in Advance:

Tickets: Purchase tickets online ahead of time to avoid long lines and save on prices. Consider a Park-to-Park ticket for flexibility if you plan to visit both parks in one day.

Reservations: Book your dining reservations in advance, especially for popular restaurants like The Leaky Cauldron or Emeril's at CityWalk.

Fast Passes: Take advantage of the Express Pass to skip regular lines for most rides. This can save a lot of time, especially on busy days.

2. Stay Hydrated and Comfortable:

Florida can be hot and humid, so bring a water bottle and refill it throughout the day. You can find free water at any quick-service restaurant.

Wear comfortable shoes for walking long distances. You'll be on your feet all day, so good footwear is essential.

3. Be Prepared for the Weather:

Florida's weather can change rapidly, especially in summer. Bring a rain poncho or an umbrella, as afternoon thunderstorms are common.

In the colder months, while the weather can be mild, consider packing a light jacket for the evenings.

4. Download the Universal Orlando App:

The Universal Orlando app offers up-to-date park information, including ride wait times, show schedules, interactive maps, and mobile food ordering.

Download it ahead of time to maximize convenience while navigating the park.

5. Arrive Early:

Arriving early allows you to take advantage of fewer crowds, especially for popular rides like Harry Potter and the Forbidden Journey or The Incredible Hulk Coaster.

If you're staying on-site, take advantage of Early Park Admission to get into the parks before they officially open.

6. Pack Light:

Keep your essentials in a small backpack or waist pack to make it easier to move around. Don't bring bulky items, as it can be cumbersome on rides and during long walks.

You can rent lockers for storing your belongings during rides, especially for attractions that require you to stow personal items (e.g., water rides or roller coasters).

7. Maximize Your Time:

Focus on high-priority attractions first (especially if you have Express Pass or are there during low crowd times).

Take breaks in the afternoon when it's hottest, and plan some indoor shows or dining experiences to rest and cool off.

8. Budget for Souvenirs:

Souvenirs at Universal can be tempting, but they can also be pricey. Set a budget for souvenirs and try to purchase them at the end of the day, so you're not carrying them around all day.

Some items are exclusive to Universal Orlando, so consider these for a unique gift or memory.

9. Know Your Health and Safety Information:

Make sure you know where the first-aid stations are located within the park. Universal Orlando Resort also has guest services available for assistance in emergencies.

If you have any dietary restrictions or allergies, be sure to check the allergen-friendly options at restaurants or notify staff as needed.

10. Have Fun and Be Flexible:

While planning is important, don't forget to leave room for spontaneity. Enjoy the fun atmosphere, try out new attractions, and take time to soak in the experience.

Be open to changes in the schedule, as weather or ride closures may impact your plans.

Useful Contacts:

Universal Orlando Resort Customer Service: +1 (407) 224-4233

Lost and Found: +1 (407) 224-4233 (Option 6)

First Aid: Available at each park, ask guest services for locations.

By following these tips, you'll ensure a smoother, more enjoyable visit to Universal Orlando Resort, and make the most out of your time there!

Themed itineraries (family, adventure, solo). Give equally the Locations, costs, contacts, etiquettes

Here are themed itineraries for different types of travelers at Universal Orlando Resort:

1. Family Itinerary

Day 1: Universal Studios Florida & Islands of Adventure

Morning:

Universal Studios Florida

Must-See: The Wizarding World of Harry Potter – Diagon Alley, Despicable Me Minion Mayhem, and E.T. Adventure.

Cost: Tickets for 1-day access range from $109-$159 per person (depending on the season).

Contact: +1 (407) 363-8000

Etiquette: Maintain a slow pace, especially in crowds. Be patient with younger children and allow extra time for stroller parking.

Afternoon:

Lunch: Eat at the Leaky Cauldron (Harry Potter-themed).

Must-See: Shrek 4D and the Wizarding World of Harry Potter – Hogsmeade.

Cost: Lunch for a family of four could range from $40-$80.

Evening:

Dinner: Have a family-friendly dinner at Bubba Gump Shrimp Co.

Must-See: The nighttime show Universal's Cinematic Celebration.

Cost: Dinner could range from $50-$100, depending on family size.

2. Adventure Itinerary

Day 1: Thrills & Rides

Morning:

Islands of Adventure

Must-See: The Incredible Hulk Coaster, Jurassic Park River Adventure, and The Amazing Adventures of Spider-Man.

Cost: Theme park tickets start at $109 for 1-day, single-park admission.

Contact: +1 (407) 363-8000

Etiquette: Use Express Pass if available to skip long lines for the best rides. Dress appropriately for water rides, and avoid carrying too many items.

Afternoon:

Lunch: Eat at Mythos Restaurant (fine dining with a view).

Must-See: Skull Island: Reign of Kong and Doctor Doom's Fearfall.

Cost: Average cost for lunch is $20-$40 per person.

Evening:

Dinner: The Cowfish Sushi Burger Bar in CityWalk for a unique twist on sushi and burgers.

Must-See: Universal's Cinematic Celebration to end your adventurous day.

Cost: Dinner averages around $50-$75 per person.

3. Solo Traveler Itinerary

Day 1: Explore at Your Own Pace

Morning:

Universal Studios Florida

Must-See: The Wizarding World of Harry Potter – Diagon Alley, Rip Ride Rockit, and Revenge of the Mummy.

Cost: 1-day single-park ticket is approximately $109.

Contact: +1 (407) 363-8000

Etiquette: Take time to soak in details of attractions like the Harry Potter areas. As a solo traveler, don't be afraid to ask staff for recommendations or directions.

Afternoon:

Lunch: Try Finnegan's Bar & Grill for a quick bite.

Must-See: Experience shows like The Bourne Stuntacular or the Blues Brothers Show.

Cost: Solo lunch will be around $15-$25.

Evening:

Dinner: Dine at VIVO Italian Kitchen in CityWalk.

Must-See: Enjoy Universal CityWalk's nightlife or relax at The Toothsome Chocolate Emporium for a treat.

Cost: Dinner and dessert will range from $25-$45.

General Tips for All Itineraries:

Location: Universal Orlando Resort is located at 6000 Universal Blvd, Orlando, FL 32819.

Costs: Tickets for 1-day access range from $109 to $159, depending on park choices and season.

Contact: +1 (407) 363-8000

Etiquette:

Respect the park's rules and regulations for safety and enjoyment.

Be courteous in lines and towards fellow visitors, especially during high-traffic times.

Stay hydrated and wear sunscreen throughout the day.

Keep the park clean by disposing of trash properly and using recycling bins when possible.

This comprehensive set of itineraries ensures that visitors can have tailored experiences based on family, adventure, or solo interests while ensuring a smooth, enjoyable visit to Universal Orlando Resort.

Checklist for travelers (packing, documents, etc.)

Here's a comprehensive checklist for travelers heading to Universal Orlando Resort:

Packing Checklist:

1. Clothing

Comfortable walking shoes

Weather-appropriate clothes (light layers, rain poncho, or jacket)

Swimsuit (if visiting water parks)

Hat, sunglasses, and sunscreen

Comfortable socks and activewear for rides

2. Essentials

Passport/ID (if traveling from abroad)

Travel tickets (printed or digital)

Park tickets (ensure you have your Universal Orlando tickets ready)

Hotel reservation and accommodation details

Travel insurance details (check for coverage related to health, rides, and cancellations)

Credit/debit cards (ensure they're valid for international use if necessary)

Emergency contacts list

Copies of important documents (stored separately for safety)

3. Health & Personal Care

Personal hygiene items (toothbrush, toothpaste, etc.)

Medications (if required)

Hand sanitizer

Portable phone charger (for a long day at the parks)

First aid kit (band-aids, antiseptic wipes)

Anti-motion sickness remedies (if you're sensitive to rides)

Wet wipes or tissue packs

4. Electronics

Smartphone with navigation apps (Google Maps, Universal Orlando App)

Charging cables, power banks

Camera or GoPro for photos and videos

Universal Orlando App for ride times, dining, and interactive maps

5. For the Kids (if applicable)

Stroller (rentals available in the park)

Snacks and water bottles

Favorite toys, books, or comfort items

Extra clothing for messes

Child safety wristbands (write down your contact details)

Documents and Travel Essentials:

1. Flight Information

Flight booking confirmation

Airline boarding passes (digital or printed)

Passport (for international travel) or a valid ID

Visa (if necessary)

Travel Insurance (ensure it covers unexpected cancellations, accidents, or emergencies)

2. Accommodation Details

Hotel confirmation number and address

Check-in and check-out times

Resort amenities and contact information

Parking information (if renting a car)

3. Park Tickets

Printed or digital Universal Orlando tickets

Park-to-Park Passes (if visiting multiple parks in a day)

VIP Experience or Express Pass tickets (if applicable)

4. Money and Payment

Credit cards (and notify the bank of travel plans to avoid fraud alerts)

Cash (for smaller purchases, tips)

Travel money cards (if preferred)

International SIM card or data roaming for mobile use

5. Health and Safety

Travel medical insurance information

Emergency contact numbers (hospital, local embassy)

Vaccination record (if required by health regulations)

6. Miscellaneous

Travel guide or Universal Orlando Resort map

Park planner with ride schedules, restaurant reservations

Reusable water bottle (filling stations are available in the parks)

Snacks and dietary supplements (if needed)

Final Travel Tips:

Arrive early: To maximize your time in the parks, arrive before opening.

Know your ride preferences: Some rides may have height and age restrictions.

Check for special events: Make sure you know the schedule for parades, shows, or seasonal events.

Weather check: Orlando can be hot and humid, so prepare for rain and pack light layers.

With this checklist, you'll be fully prepared for your Universal Orlando Resort adventure, ensuring a stress-free and enjoyable experience!

Basic Questions for Every Traveler

1. Months Before Departure/ At the Time of Booking

1. Do I have a passport? Is it still valid?

No international travel essential list is possible without a passport.

If you are traveling overseas for the first time, ensure you have a passport. If you don't have one yet, apply immediately since the process can take about 4 – 6 weeks.

If you have traveled overseas before, you will certainly have a passport. All you have to do is check its validity.

Most of the countries require at least 6 month's validity along with a few blank pages left beyond your stay. If your passport is about to expire soon, it's better to renew it so that the visa process can begin.

2. Do I need a Visa?

As crucial as the passport, Visa is another travel essential for an overseas trip. Once you have shortlisted your destination, it is important to check its visa requirement as the process can take somewhere around a week to a month. Some countries may even grant you a visa on arrival. It all depends on the country you are from and the country you are going to.

3. Are there any required vaccinations?

Once you have shortlisted your destination, go through the list of recommended travel immunizations for that country to move forward on the travel essentials list.

Talk to your doctor about necessary travel vaccinations. It is important to complete this as soon as possible since it can take a few weeks for immunizations to come into play and build strong immunity.

Also, carry the certificate of vaccinations done as in some cases you may be asked to show them during immigration.

4. Where will I be staying?

Planning ahead makes you a smart traveler. Once your ticket and visa are done, it is a good idea to search through your destination and shortlist hotels/resorts/air-bnbs. Not only will it help you conclude an important part of your packing for vacation but also get you easy availability/early bird discount especially if it is a peak season time.

5. Do I need a guidebook?

While some may say, why buy a guidebook when everything is easily available online, **NEWMAN S. JACKSON** is still worth the money as it is one of the most comprehensive stores of reliable travel info. From the things you may have googled to the things, you may have forgotten to native emergency numbers to all the hidden cafes and hostels to tipping etiquettes. You will never miss any info especially if your phone dies or is in airplane mode.

6. Do I need an International Driving Permit?

If you are planning to rent a car/bike on your trip, it will be a travel essential to get an international driving permit. The rules differ from country to country so do your research and apply well in time.

2. Month Before Departure

7. Should I get Travel Insurance?

Travelling to a new country, far away from home can bring in a lot of what-ifs to the mind which can lead to nervousness. To be on the safer side, it is always better to add insurance to your travel essentials list.

Check with your credit card companies as sometimes it is included and if it is not, opt for a travel insurance that is easy, affordable and hassle-free.

Better safe than sorry.

8. Have I re-confirmed hotel/transport bookings?

It is always better to reconfirm and check all the hotel or regional transport bookings, shuttle buses etc. done when packing for vacation. Take printouts and store them in one folder for easy maneuvering through last-minute packing.

9. How will I access local currency?

An important thing to pack for international travel along with credit/cash/debit card is some local currency. You can either get some from your bank or a trusted travel agent or even at the airport although the exchange rates aren't the best there.

10. Do I need to arrange for a house/pet sitting?

If you live alone or are traveling with the whole family make sure your home/pet is taken care of while you are busy packing for vacation. You can either talk to a trusted friend or arrange a professional. Always better than hurrying at the last moment.

3. Week Before Departure

11. Have I made copies of all travel essential documents?

Since your departure date is just a week after, it is better to make copies of all important international travel essential documents: passport, visa, insurance itineraries, flight tickets, and hotel reservations. Leave this folder with a trusted friend. Also, take pictures of all travel essential documents while making copies and keep them in your google drive or email account. The idea is to have easy access to them in case you somehow lose them.

12. What is my airline carry on and luggage policy?

It is important to be aware of airplane luggage rules when packing for vacation as they are strict and keep changing. It is advisable to go through your airlines' guidelines thoroughly, to see things to pack for international travel in your check-in and cabin bags. Also, keep in mind the weight limit of check-in/cabin bags while packing so as to avoid any excess fees.

13. Do I need a cell phone plan?

An important international travel essential is an apt cell phone plan as the last thing you want to do as you reach your destination country is run and worry about how to get your phone on a working network. You can either get a plan activated on your existing network or take an exclusive international calling card or take a prepaid Sim card with the data/call plan from the airport as soon as you land. Go through all the options while packing for vacation, see which one is the best on the features and lightest on the pocket and choose accordingly.

14. Do I need an International travel charger?

It may not be necessary that the charging ports of your destination country are the same as yours. Always do your research while packing for vacation and invest in a universal travel adapter - international travel essential.

15. Have I packed in the essentials?

Traveling smart requires packing which may not be the most fun thing to do but definitely one of the most important. While wondering about things to pack for international travel, don't forget to pack light, add clothes according to the weather, necessary medicines, eye mask, and earplugs.

16. Is there inflight entertainment?

The best way to pass time in a long haul flight after conversations and sleeping is inflight entertainment. Check your flight for their inflight status and also download some backup entertainment on your device or carry a good book to binge-watch on the airport or in case the inflight entertainment isn't working.

17. Have I refilled my medicines/prescriptions?

While packing for vacation, do not forget to carry travel essential medicines, the ones you need in routine and ones for regular ailments such as flu, a stomach infection, fever, etc. Also, carry a prescription of all the medicines that you are carrying in case they decide to check at immigration.

4. Day Before Departure

18. Can I check-in for my flight online?

The online check-in usually opens 24 hours before the flight. It is always advisable to do an online check-in as not only you get your favorite seats but you also avoid standing in long queues and save time.

19. Have I weighed my luggage?

Once you are finishing up packing for vacation, weigh in your luggage again. Keep in mind the luggage limit allowed by your airlines to avoid any extra fee while checking in.

20. Have I checked all my electronics?

Check-in all your electronics, their battery status, space on memory cards, etc. as the last thing you want is being stuck without electronics and not being able to connect with family or take pictures.

21. Have I packed everything on my packing for the vacation list?

Run through your packing list once, double-checking everything you planned to take with you. From toiletries to makeup to charger – recheck every travel essential item.

22. Have I confirmed my flight status?

Before leaving home, make sure your flight is running on time.

23. Do I have all my travel essential documents?

Another important thing to check before leaving home, check if you have all important documents and their copy if any need arises

24. Have I arranged my ride to the airport?

Make sure you have booked a cab or told you, family and friends, to be ready and reach the airport at least 3 and a half hours before your flight.

25. Do I have enough local/destination currency?

While leaving, make sure you have some local currency in your wallet, since you may need to book a cab, buy water or a local sim card at the airport

DATE:
_____

20 _ _

DURATION:

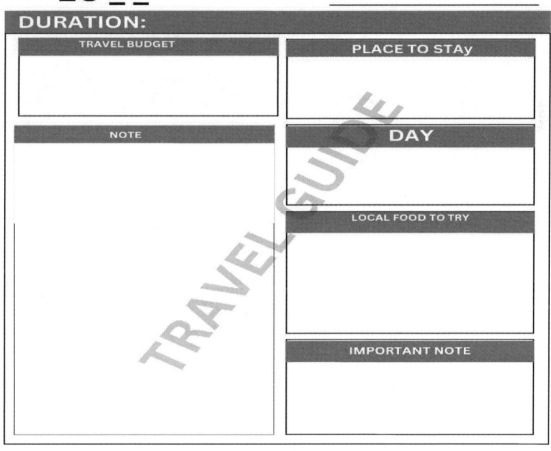

TRAVEL BUDGET	PLACE TO STAy

NOTE	DAY
	LOCAL FOOD TO TRY
	IMPORTANT NOTE

TRAVEL & TOUR GUIDE JOURNAL

20 _ _

DATE:
_____

DURATION:

TRAVEL BUDGET

PLACE TO STAy

NOTE

DAY

LOCAL FOOD TO TRY

IMPORTANT NOTE

TRAVEL GUIDE

TRAVEL & TOUR GUIDE JOURNAL

DATE:

_____

20 _ _

DURATION:

TRAVEL BUDGET

PLACE TO STAy

NOTE

DAY

LOCAL FOOD TO TRY

IMPORTANT NOTE

TRAVEL GUIDE

TRAVEL & TOUR GUIDE JOURNAL

20 _ _

DATE:
_____

DURATION:

TRAVEL BUDGET

PLACE TO STAy

NOTE

DAY

LOCAL FOOD TO TRY

IMPORTANT NOTE

TRAVEL GUIDE

TRAVEL & TOUR GUIDE JOURNAL

DATE:

20 _ _

DURATION:

TRAVEL BUDGET

PLACE TO STAy

NOTE

DAY

LOCAL FOOD TO TRY

IMPORTANT NOTE

TRAVEL GUIDE

TRAVEL & TOUR GUIDE JOURNAL

20 _ _

DATE:
_____

DURATION:

TRAVEL BUDGET

PLACE TO STAy

NOTE

DAY

LOCAL FOOD TO TRY

IMPORTANT NOTE

TRAVEL GUIDE

TRAVEL & TOUR GUIDE JOURNAL

DATE:
_____

20 _ _

DURATION:

TRAVEL BUDGET

PLACE TO STAy

NOTE

DAY

LOCAL FOOD TO TRY

IMPORTANT NOTE

TRAVEL & TOUR GUIDE JOURNAL

DATE:

20 _ _

DURATION:

TRAVEL BUDGET

PLACE TO STAy

NOTE

DAY

LOCAL FOOD TO TRY

IMPORTANT NOTE

TRAVEL GUIDE

TRAVEL & TOUR GUIDE JOURNAL

20 _ _

DATE:
_____

DURATION:

TRAVEL BUDGET

PLACE TO STAy

NOTE

DAY

LOCAL FOOD TO TRY

IMPORTANT NOTE

TRAVEL GUIDE

TRAVEL & TOUR GUIDE JOURNAL

DATE:
_____

20 _ _

DURATION:

TRAVEL BUDGET

PLACE TO STAy

NOTE

DAY

LOCAL FOOD TO TRY

IMPORTANT NOTE

TRAVEL GUIDE

Made in the USA
Columbia, SC
11 February 2025

53705715R00063